W9-DBA-275

Don't Wish You Had,
Be Glad You Did

Don't Wish You Had, Be Glad You Did

A Look at Life by
Jud Ammons with Adam Lucas

Illustrations by George Doles, III

Pentland Press, Inc.
www.pentlandpressusa.com

PUBLISHED BY PENTLAND PRESS, INC.
5122 Bur Oak Circle, Raleigh, North Carolina 27612
United States of America
919-782-0281

ISBN 1-57197-246-3
Library of Congress Control Number 00-134887

Printed in the United States of America

Table of Contents

Introduction

Any time someone becomes a success, the immediate expectation is that luck played an important part. Even with Raleigh developer Jud Ammons, that holds true. One newspaper reporter quoted his brother as saying, "Jud could flip up a nickel and it would come down a quarter."

That might be true. But while the nickel was in the air, he'd be doing everything he knew how to do to turn it into a quarter. And if it came down a quarter, he'd immediately begin thinking about how to turn it into a fifty-cent piece.

That dedication has won him numerous awards, too many to list. Enter his office, which is located just off the kitchen in his house, and you'll find Homebuilder of the Year awards piled on top of Excellence in Design awards in the corner, just under a framed cartoon of Jud wearing a Richard Petty hat.

Ask him about his awards, however, and he's likely to bring up some of the championships his dogs have won at field trials. He's developed land from the mountains to the ocean, but he'd prefer to talk about his dogs. It's that attitude that often makes people meeting him for the first time assume that he is a simple country boy. Once they get to know him, they quickly learn the truth. The difference between the first impression and the truth makes Jud Ammons a memorable person to all of his acquaintances.

His oldest son, Andy, remembers a recent conversation with an architect. "I had a meeting with a man that was going to work on some houses for us. I had never met him before, but as we began talking, he realized that I was Jud's son. He was just beside himself. He said, 'Did your dad really think that house over in the development I worked on was the prettiest he had ever seen?'

"I had no idea what the guy was talking about. But it turned out that about ten years ago, Dad had been quoted in the paper saying that a specific house was the prettiest he had seen. The architect didn't know Dad, but he had remembered that quote for ten years."

It's not easy to pinpoint what makes him so memorable. A cynical person might say it's because he's not afraid to express his opinion in a loud and bombastic fashion, but truthfully, he has mellowed over the past few years. A more gullible person might say that it's because Jud is simple, that he rides around in a pickup truck and has a van for long trips. That's not quite accurate, either. The word "simple" implies a cluelessness that is completely inaccurate.

In truth, it's a combination of those two factors that make him what he is. Most importantly, there is absolutely no pretense with him. When he asked me to work on this book, an associate told me that at least I wouldn't have to worry about whether or not he liked me. If he didn't, he would tell me to my face that he thought I was lazy and a slacker.

Underneath that gruff exterior, there's a loving family man. Not everyone gets the chance to see the way he cares for his wife, Jo Ellen, or the way he talks about his grandchildren. His desire to help people is often overshadowed by his mammoth developing projects, but his close friends know what goes on beyond closed doors.

"The account of his career as an entrepreneur is only one aspect of Jud's life," friend Caralie Brown says. "Listening to a grandson talk about fishing with his grandfather or hearing a granddaughter call, 'I'm going with you,' as she leaves the church, are glimpses of a close relationship with his grandchildren.

"Having people whom Jud has helped to form their own companies work in my yard and in my home has shown me that Jud wants others to learn from his principles and to succeed as entrepreneurs."

Brown goes on to point out how involved her friend has been with Greystone Baptist Church, from the building stages to serving as a deacon. Most people don't know just how involved he has actually been, and he won't allow it to be revealed in these pages. He has never received credit for all the attempts he makes to help people because he doesn't want credit for it. More correctly, unlike some people, he doesn't need credit for it. When he goes out of his way for someone, he does it not for the publicity it might generate, but because it makes him feel good and he likes to see people succeed.

One of his closest friends, Jim Seay, says that the most important part of Jud's personality is that he's a survivor. He's survived and flourished through growing up in the mountains, starting his own business, and the useless nuisance of an IRS audit.

Despite his success, he remains as accessible as ever. His favorite newspaper article written about him was entitled, "A Country Boy with a Magic Touch." Some people might be offended by the connotations of the words "country boy." Jud considers them a compliment.

That's the attitude that I hope is revealed in this book. It's a long trip from selling pigs in the mountains of North Carolina to developing four hundred acres of land at Nags Head. What makes Jud's story special is that he enjoyed the journey from point to point as much as the final destination—even though he still, in my opinion, hasn't made it to the finish.

—Adam Lucas

Prologue

I've always tried to be a doer, not a talker. It bothers me when all people want to do is sit around and talk about what they *could* do or *would* do if they had a chance. If they'd quit talking about it and get out and actually do it, then maybe they'd get a little more accomplished. My wife, Jo Ellen, and I have tried to instill that same feeling in our four children, Andy, David, Jeff, and Alma.

I think that's why my family was surprised that it took me so long to start this book. For a long time, I'd often say, "I'm going to put this in my book." The problem was, I never actually started. Finally, one day Andy came into my office and slapped down a Dictaphone with a cash register receipt taped to it. He told me that I could either use it to write my book or I could take it back. Either way, he said he wanted to quit hearing about my book. If I wrote it, he wanted to read it when I was finished, but if I took the Dictaphone back to the store, then I had to be quiet about it. After I got to thinking about it, there were a lot of reasons to go ahead with the writing.

Why did I decide to write the book? For one thing, my kids have encouraged me to do it for my grandkids. Somebody said that the only thing in the world not overrated is grandchildren. I've decided that if there are two things in the world that aren't overrated, one of them is becoming a Christian. The other thing is grandchildren.

If there's any way that writing a book will help my grandchildren do any better in the future, it'll be worth it.

I've tried to avoid coming across as a know-it-all and a pessimist. I think my vast experiences have allowed me to learn many lessons the hard way, but I know that I don't know everything. I'm an optimist. Most people think I'm the most optimistic person they know. I'm a long way from being a pessimist. It's even obvious by the way I answer the phone. People will call me and say, "How are you doing?" My response is always, "The best in the world." I always feel like that's the truth. Anybody who makes a living signing personal loans for land that he doesn't even know if he can develop certainly can't be a pessimist. I guess I have a short memory, because no matter what troubles we go through to get a permit or something related to government red tape, I only think about all the pretty things we can build.

That doesn't mean that I don't see when things are bad and going to get worse. When I talk about things that are bad, it's just because I'd like to figure out a way to improve them or encourage someone else to improve them. Unless it's pointed out to people that something is being done badly, they usually don't even realize it. They get so used to the usual routine that they don't even stop to think about it.

I operate on the assumption that I owe it to myself, my family, and my business to abide by as many rules as I have to in order to make my projects work and meet the requirements set down by government agencies. However, I strongly believe that I owe it to myself not to pretend that I like anything if I don't like it. I take it very seriously that I should help change the things I don't like.

Although we have dabbled in a lot of different projects, the sky was the limit on how many we could have done. Through the years, I have elected to do challenging and beneficial projects rather than just moneymaking projects. I have always been concerned about getting bigger and doing more, which meant less hands-on work, more management, and more time spent with bankers, lawyers, regulators, and those types of people. Fewer projects meant I could supervise on the job and incorporate my personal touch. Fewer projects allowed me to spend time with the action, working with people like bulldozer operators, carpenters, and landscapers. Those were my kind of people and I felt I was effective working with them. It hasn't always worked out that way, but I have enjoyed being in the field making things happen.

I hope and pray that the people who read this book will not be just the ones who had experiences similar to mine. They probably know more about what I'm talking about than I do. I want the vast majority of people to be the ones who never had the thrill of being in their own business, of taking a risk, and making something happen on their own. I know that not everyone sold pigs in the mountains, as I talk about in the first chapter, but the main point of that story isn't that selling pigs builds character; it's that hard work pays off. I wish more people would rather be broke and starting over than scared to take a chance.

My entire family has been a great help and encouragement to me in writing this book. They have always understood that I live by what I have written in the following pages. I've had many friends, business associates, and employees who have helped me form many of my opinions along the way. In that fashion, they have also been a big help with this book. I didn't try to make a detailed list of the friends who have helped me. I hope that no one will either feel left out or be glad that they were left out.

Chapter 1

Thrashers, Figs, and Regret

When I was growing up, we lived way up in the mountains north of Asheville, North Carolina near the Tennessee state line. We lived on a farm and I think most people would say that we lived way out in the country. I had three brothers and three sisters, but one of my sisters died when she was little. I was right in the middle as far as age goes. We weren't poor, but we had to work hard for what we had. People did what they had to do to make a decent living. Even though we worked hard, I remember how happy we were and how happy I was.

When I was young, my dad rented some land, like a tenant farmer, plus he owned a little bit of land. He was always trying to make progress by buying more land. Earlier than that, during the Depression, he had to go off and work for the forest service or other public works and wasn't around home much. We'd have to take care of the farm when he wasn't there because times were real bad back in the late '30s and early '40s. There was no money to hire extra help. You learned early on to take responsibility and you did what you had to do. It wasn't a matter of being told what to do. You looked for something to do. Doing your part was expected. We'd get up in the morning and work for one or two hours before we'd eat breakfast. On days that we had school, we did at least one hour of our work before we went to school. We didn't even really consider it work. It was just part of daily life.

Sometimes you remember little bits of things from when you were young, but you don't know if you're remembering what people have told you or if you really are remembering what happened. If you look at pictures long enough, you start to feel like you were actually there when they were taken. For example, I had two sisters and a brother older than me and two brothers and a sister younger than me. My little sister, who was about a year younger than me, died when I was about six years old. Sometimes I think I remember her and other times I'm not sure. My older sisters always tell me about her and I've seen pictures of her. I'm never sure if I'm remembering the pictures, the stories I've been told, or my own memories of her.

My mother used to tell the story that when I started school I didn't want to leave home and I cried quite a bit. After two days of this, they let my little sister go to school with me for about three weeks so that I would go without crying. It was only three or four months after that that she died. She had diphtheria. Back then you didn't go to the hospital when you got sick. It's hard when you're six years old and someone that has been a part of your whole life suddenly isn't there anymore. Six-year-olds don't understand death. I'm not even sure that sixty-year-olds do either.

Times were still tough then and the war was just starting. We didn't have a TV or radio or even lights because there was no electricity. Soon after that, we did get electricity, but it wasn't like we think of today. We take it for granted that you walk into a room, flip the switch, and you've got all the light you need. Our idea of electricity was one bare bulb hanging down from the ceiling on a cord. You'd pull the cord and the bulb would shine brightly right in your eyes. I can still remember squinting into that light.

Not long after we got electricity, we also got a radio. After school, I listened to "The Lone Ranger and His Pal Tonto." Today it seems like radio is an afterthought. If you can't watch the ballgame on television, then you feel like you're missing something if you have to listen on the radio. But back then it was a really big deal.

I hardly remember that the war went on. We were kind of isolated up in the mountains. I started hearing about some of the boys in our community getting killed. Mothers in the town would be so upset. There would always be a memorial service at the church. One family we knew had two of their boys killed.

As I've said, we rented a little land, but it wasn't enough to make a very good living. At the time, it was hard to make decent money. A lot of people were unemployed. The government started CCC camps, the Civilian Conservation Corps. They also had WPA, Work Projects Administration, at the time. The people who worked at the CCC camps would clean up road banks, plant trees in steep areas, things like that. One of the most famous scenic routes in the country, the Blue Ridge Parkway, was built by the CCC project. Even now, you can see the evidence of things they did.

We had a CCC camp on my granddad's property, behind my house. It was kind of interesting, because they had a lot of buildings. There were probably about 250 people living there. I'm now developing a subdivision on some of that family land and we're pushing up some of those old water lines. I had to take up some of the concrete where the washhouse was.

We'd pick up the food left over from the meals all the men would eat. That's what we'd feed our hogs. That led to the first time and probably the only time I remember my daddy crying.

We must have had about one hundred or two hundred hogs. The leftover food from the CCC camps was a dirty mess, but at least the hogs would eat it and it was cheaper than buying food. People hear the word "hogs" and think of these big old dirty animals, but they weren't just hogs to us—they were part of our livelihood. Anything that helped make money was a huge deal in those days, because it was so difficult to find a way to earn a living.

One time our hogs got cholera. It was such a bad disease. I remember walking up with my father to that big green field where all the hogs were. It was hard to figure out what was going on, but as you stood there and looked, you noticed the hogs were all lying down in an odd configuration with their legs crossed. Every single one of our hogs was dead within two days.

People in today's society might think it was silly to stand there and cry over hogs, like my father did. But he wasn't just crying over hogs. We had raised those hogs for nearly a year and counted on them for part of our income. When your hogs die, it's not a fixable problem. It's not like having a delivery service and your truck breaks down. If that happens, you just go get your truck fixed. But you can't bring your hogs back.

Sometimes when interest rates get high or something else affects our business, I start to think it's bad. But then I remember that it's nothing compared to those hogs. At least when rates get high, I know that I made something last year and hope to make something next year and that this year is only part of the picture. Those hogs were about all that we had and they all lay dead. To make matters worse, we had to dig holes to bury them all, hundreds of holes in our land with our income buried inside them. People today think it's a big risk to put a little bit of money in the stock market. Back then we had a different idea of risk. It meant putting all your faith and money into hogs and then being forced to see them sprawled out dead across the field.

My dad didn't want to work with the CCC camps. He wanted to work for the forest service, because he thought that was a better job. He worked over near Mount Mitchell and was gone a lot. One Christmas when he came home, it was almost like a story that you would see on TV. We weren't sure when he was coming, because people couldn't communicate then like they do now. It's not like my son, who has a beeper tied to a satellite and all that stuff.

My dad came home on Christmas Eve with presents in his arms, and it was snowing, just like you would picture it. People might say that movies that turn out that way are corny, but that's because they've never experienced it in real life. You don't want to spend the holidays without your family and to see my father walking through that snow with those presents really made me feel good.

That Christmas we planned to go to Asheville and see the first movie any of us had seen. I was seven or eight. We all piled in the pickup truck and went to Asheville (which was a big city to us) to see *Snow White and the Seven Dwarfs*.

My dad and my mother had to work really hard. My mother 's dad didn't drive, and she didn't drive either, so she stayed home and worked all the time. From time to time, we hired people to work on our farm and she'd always cook for those people. Anything you thought you had to have, she could make for you. They'd come up to the house all the time. My mother used to fix lunch for sometimes ten to fifteen people. Ours was a place where people sort of gathered around.

I remember when the thrashers used to come around. Now there are big combines that cut the wheat. But then, we cut it by hand with what they call a cradle, which was like a scythe. We'd cut it and tie it up in bundles. The thrashing machine would come around once a year to separate the wheat from the straw. It took eight or ten men to run the thrashing machine. Four or five or six neighbors would get together and help each other thrash. We'd thrash one farm and then move on to the next one. The man with the machine would just bring it along from farm to farm. We did a lot of things that way.

When the thrashers came, there would be three or four days where my mother would fix lunch for fifteen or twenty people. There was always a big crowd, but it didn't seem to bother her. There was never a question about whether they'd get fed. We knew that she could do it. Today if you wanted to feed that many people you'd have to go out and hire a caterer, plan for two weeks, and have a fancy menu.

My grandpa lived one hundred miles away. He was a preacher. He lived in a parsonage right by the church. Occasionally, I'd tell people I was wearing "preacher clothes," because if he wore a suit out, my mother would take what was left and make one for us when we were little. We'd take turns going down to stay with my grandparents because my mother thought it would be good for us to learn from her father.

Most of my grandpa's congregation lived within four or five miles of the parsonage so he didn't drive a car. Tuesdays and Thursdays were visiting days. When we were with him, we'd walk off in a different direction each morning, stopping along the way to meet with members of his congregation. We would eat lunch wherever we wound up. No one ever seemed to mind feeding us. I would walk with him and while he was in the house talking and ministering to people in his congregation I'd always go outside around back to where the grapes and figs were. That was how I remembered it; when it was visiting time for my grandfather, the grapes and figs would be ripe.

Some people want to know what I regret most in my life. That's a hard question to answer, because no one wants to think about the things that didn't turn out as well as he had hoped. One of the things I regret the most was that by the time I had made a little money and could help my mother, she died. She died young. She was only fifty-six years old. She had been the only one in the family that had never been sick, but she got pericarditis. Three days after she got it, she died. That was bad, because it was just getting to where I thought maybe she wouldn't have to work so hard. I never really got the chance to make life easier for her.

Now that I get older, though, I watch my kids. Watching them work hard, I realize that her seeing me work hard was the good part. My middle son, David, said he didn't want to be in the building business. He said all he remembered about it was that when he got up I was on the phone looking for a plumber, and when he went to bed at night I was at the drafting table drawing plans. At the time my mother died, I thought that she missed the good part, but now I realize that she saw it. The good part was when I was working to do it, not when I was enjoying it. I'm sure my mother felt that way, even though I didn't get to give her everything I would have liked. That's one of those things that I've learned with experience.

I've been fortunate, because I've had two mothers that were very good influences, my own mother and the mother of my wife, Jo Ellen. She was such an inspiration to us. She taught Sunday school even after she lost her eyesight. She had to order the material on tape so that she could listen to it and be able to teach it.

We make fun of kids now that go to rock concerts and scream. Older people like to pretend that they would never do anything that silly. But things haven't changed that much. I remember going to Asheville one time for a show. The Asheville City Auditorium was like the little Grand Ole Opry. Once I saw a concert there. Hank Williams, Sr. was coming, and it was right before he died. His was just the biggest show ever. It was comparable to Elvis Presley coming to town in the 1960s. I thought I had to look sharp and my girlfriend was going to dress up. My mother made me a pair of red pants out of some stuff she had and she put a yellow stripe down the side of them. It sounds silly, but I really thought I was fancy. Kids haven't changed much now from what they were then. They still like to go and holler and scream and girls act like they're going to faint.

My mother used to make our suits. Back then you didn't buy many things. Most things we had on the farm but there'd be a few things you'd have to buy like sugar and dry beans. We'd also buy some kind of high protein mix to put in the livestock feed. We'd milk the cows and sell some of the milk and butter. When we'd go buy the feed, my sisters wanted to go with my dad to help pick out the sacks. They did this because back then they'd put the feed in real flowery feed sacks.

We bought the feed and after the sack was empty it was still good for something. If you were real careful when you washed it, Mother could make clothes and dresses out of those feed sacks. My sisters were proud to wear them because they'd have about the best looking dresses of anyone around. It probably sounds strange to people reading this to think that they were proud to wear feed sacks, but we were just making the best out of our situation. I'm no fashion expert, but it seems to me that most of today's dresses don't look much better than the ones my sisters used to wear.

We didn't always have running water in our house. Eventually, though, we finally got water to come from a spigot on the back porch. It was sort of like the deal with electricity in that it wasn't anything like what we have today. At the time, though, it was really good. When we took a bath, we still had to carry the water in a pan and heat it or else we just took a cold bath. It was better than what we had had, but it was nothing to write home about. We would put the tub in the corner of the bedroom to take our baths. Before this, we had to go outside to bathe, so if it was cold you didn't take many baths. Going outside in those cold mountain winters to take a bath was not a pleasant proposition. Even if it wasn't too cold, you had to build a fire to heat the water out there in the yard.

At the same time we got running water, we also got an inside toilet, which meant we had to have a septic tank in the yard. When we finally got a bathroom, we thought we were something. These days when you're building houses you've got to have three bathrooms and an extra one in case guests come. We had all those kids in the house and we just had the one bathroom and we were so proud to have that.

The beds for all the kids were in one room. One year, though, Dad built a garage with rooms over the top out by the woodshed and smokehouse. The girls were thirteen or fourteen and by then I was eight or nine. Our parents thought we were too old to be sleeping in the same room. The rooms my dad built above the garage and woodshed were where the boys slept.

We thought we were lucky because we had a room apiece, but we didn't have any running water or a bathroom in our place above the garage. We had one light overhead. It was about twenty or thirty feet to the house, where we had to take our bath. You could really get your speed up in the wintertime going out there. I'm surprised I didn't turn out to be an Olympic sprinter with all the practicing I did, hurrying from the tub to my room across the yard. Our rooms didn't have any heat so Mother used to heat a metal iron behind the stove, or we had a brick we'd heat behind the stove or at the fireplace. We'd wrap that up in a little blanket and carry it with us and throw it in the bed and put our feet on it. But no matter what you did at night, when you hopped up in the morning it was about as bad as it ever was.

Since we didn't have any heat and we liked the fresh air, we'd sometimes leave the windows open even in the winter. Snow would blow in the windows. I slept all those years without any heat. We got to where we liked it. We had killed a sheep to eat one time, so I took the sheepskin and dried it out. I laid that down to hop on in the morning when I climbed out of bed. I thought I had died and gone to heaven, it felt so good.

We didn't have a freezer to keep things cold, even though sometimes we felt like we could've just sat something in our room to freeze it. We kept the milk in a box where we could run cold water over it. Some people's water supply was pretty far away from their house.

Because of this they would use a "lazy girl," which was a bucket that would run down on a wire one hundred or two hundred feet to where the water was. That would save you walking up and down the hill all the time. We didn't have one of those, but that was the first time I ever started thinking about mechanical things. I loved to work on stuff like that.

Because we didn't have refrigeration, if you killed anything to eat, you either had to eat it in a hurry, can it, or it had to be cold weather. If it was chilly, we could put it in the smokehouse. When you killed a pig, you'd have to put salt on top of it to keep it from spoiling. You couldn't do beef or chicken that way because you couldn't salt them down.

We always grew a lot of our own food so that we would have something to eat in the winter, but in order to keep it we had to preserve it. We canned some apples, but we dried most of them. My mother would peel and slice them and we'd lay them out on a piece of tin out on the sawhorses up about head high, which would keep the varmints from getting them. We'd leave them up there for a few days and go turn them every once in a while to make sure that both sides were dry. The sun would dry them out and we'd have apples to eat all winter so that we could make apple pies and other things.

Those delicious apples lying out there all alone sure were a temptation, though. One time I was out there sneaking me some apples and eating them. My mother didn't think that was near as funny as I did. She went out when I wasn't looking and put some red hot pepper on four or five of them so that she could catch me doing it. I thought I was being sly, but the next thing I knew my mouth was on fire. That about burnt my mess up. It made me so mad.

I thought I'd fix her. I took the ones she had peppered and peppered a few more and then scattered them among the others, so she wouldn't know where they were. I thought I'd teach her a lesson, but my dad didn't think that was funny either. I found myself out there picking up and peeling about three times as many apples to replace the ones I had messed up.

We raised chickens, too. Right after Christmas we'd get little baby chickens and keep them in the house on some old paper in front of the fireplace. After about a month, they'd start growing feathers, so then we'd have to clean the house every day. People talk about dogs shedding, but that's nothing compared to what chickens can do. We had to keep them in the house because we didn't have any other place to keep them warm. When it started warming up a little, you could put them outside. Because we kept them in the house, we'd have chickens big enough to eat before our neighbors did. Today people roll their eyes at us for having kept chickens in the house. They probably think we were just crazy old country people, but in reality it made life easier to keep them in there because they got bigger faster.

When it was time to eat, we just picked out the chicken we wanted and chopped his head off or Mother would wring his neck. Throw on some hot water, pluck it to get the feathers off, and you could eat it for lunch. Now that's what I call fresh.

My grandmother would make soap and sell it. She also made butter and three or four kinds of medicines and sold them. We'd dig ginseng and put it in things. Back then we made a joke of it, sort of like making fun of people that did things according to the almanac or the signs. It's hard to realize how much stuff we used to make back then, just thinking it was the mountain way. Today, people buy all of it at the store. The only difference in the quality is that these days, it comes in a fancy box or wrapping paper.

The base for her medicine would be the rosin off of white pine trees. At a certain time of year, before cold weather came, we had to climb tree after tree to get bucketfuls of it so she could make her medicine. She was an entrepreneur from way back.

Maybe it ran in the family, because the rest of us also did entrepreneurial-type things. We were able to make a little bit of money as a pin hooker, which is really somebody that wants to buy things. We'd go around and see someone that had a cow but didn't have a way to get it to town to sell it. We'd say, "Well, that cow weighs about eight hundred pounds and would bring thirty cents a pound, so that's $240." We'd buy it and take it to town and hope it weighed eight hundred and fifty pounds and brought thirty-four cents a pound. You could do it with cows, lumber, and especially with tobacco, which we would take just over the mountain to the auction markets in Johnson City, Tennessee. Not many people had a truck to haul things in.

In the winter, we had a business hauling tobacco for people. They wouldn't want to wait on the auction all day, so we'd just buy it from them and take it to the auction ourselves. You learned early on that you needed a keen eye to figure out how much it weighed and what it was worth. My daddy could look at a cow or horse and if he missed it more than fifteen pounds, he'd be upset. It doesn't take long to learn about making a profit in the pin hooker business. The first time you overestimate the value of a product and lose money on it, you learn that you won't be in business very long if you do it that way.

We also canned beef—filet mignon, porterhouse steaks, the whole beef. Mama always wanted half-gallon cans with large necks so that we wouldn't have to slice the meat up small to put it in there. Even now, when I go to places, I order roast beef or chop steak and they say, "Don't you want a nice steak?" Well, I'm used to the chopped steak being the filet. That was the best we had. In a way, it looks like we had it pretty tough, but we ate well.

Even before we had a refrigerator or freezer, there were ways to make do. There was a man in Asheville who built a place where you could rent freezer lockers. Then you could kill beef or something and not have to can it. He would keep it frozen for you so it wouldn't spoil. A lot of people started using freezer lockers.

I remember one Sunday after church I rode my bicycle down by the mill wheel. I was probably ten or eleven. There wasn't electricity to run the mills, so they were powered by water. That was true at a lot of places, like textile mills. We would grind our corn and wheat at the mill. For a long time, my grandpa ran a mill down by the big creek, which was several miles from where we lived. It was a very good place to go fishing, because it was dammed. I was fishing by myself and I had already caught a couple of nice fish and was feeling pretty pleased with myself.

Most of the churches in our area were Baptist churches and most didn't have a baptistery. Plus, they liked to baptize in the river because it was supposed to be symbolic, like John the Baptist. They decided to come have a baptizing in the creek. I just kept on fishing. Then they decided to baptize at the spot I was using. They started waving at me to move over from where I was fishing. This was my best fishing spot that they wanted to use. It was good for me because it was deep enough to draw the fish, and it was good for them because it was deep enough to dip someone in the water. This wasn't one of those Methodist baptizings where they just sprinkle you with a drop of water. I decided I was going to ignore them. I kept throwing my line out there. I didn't run them off, but I remember they didn't like it. They kept staring at me, and I still didn't move over. When the preacher told my daddy what had happened, it ceased to be a joke. My daddy didn't think it was nearly as funny as I did. He had a way of letting you know real fast when something wasn't funny.

One thing that I spent a lot of time with when I was around that age was my dogs. Now that I'm older, it's still my favorite hobby and the thing I spend the most time with other than work and my family. I've raised beagle dogs since the early 1960s. I spend a lot of time with them. When you've had a bad day, you can go out at four or five in the afternoon and spend two or three hours with just you and your dogs, training them in the country. It's a lot of fun. I even like it when it's rainy and dark and most people would say it's too nasty outside to do anything.

I'm sure that people who only know me from working with me can't imagine me out there with the dogs. They think, "How can old Jud, who yells and screams all the time and is always in a hurry, be quiet and patient long enough to be with his dogs when they're on the trail of something?" They don't realize that everyone has to have some time when they can think and be by themselves. That's what my dogs do for me.

When I was growing up, I always had dogs. Nobody in my family liked dogs or hunting except me. I had hound dogs and coon dogs and I'd hunt whatever my dogs would hunt. If they chased a rabbit, then I was rabbit hunting. If they chased a squirrel, then I was squirrel hunting. It wasn't so much what you were after, but the thrill of being after it.

One time I ordered me two of the nicest big old black-and-tans out of a magazine advertisement. They were the original bugle-mouth dogs, which meant that when they barked they were very loud and clear, which was very important. I was about eleven or twelve and had saved my money for a long time for those dogs. They were being sent from Indiana or Illinois and they came in on the train in a big old box. I thought they were the prettiest things I had ever seen in my life. I named one Sut and one Smut, because they were so black.

The first chance I got to run them was when my buddies wanted to go on a foxhunt up near a mountain that was close to where I lived. You have to wait until after ten o'clock at night to fox hunt because that's when the foxes come out. The men would build a fire and cook a chicken or something and let the dogs go off and chase foxes.

I didn't want to take both of my new dogs, because I was afraid I'd lose them. We were about three miles from where I lived and I was afraid they wouldn't be able to find their way home, so I just took one. Everyone turned his dogs loose and mine went with the pack. After awhile we heard a dog strike and all of them started running. You could tell by the sound of their bark which one was which. The hunters would be calling out their dogs' names when they heard them. One would say, "I heard old Rock strike," or "I hear old Blue." I wasn't exactly sure what mine sounded like, because I hadn't ever hunted with it before. But I didn't think that I heard Smut. After awhile though, we heard this strange-mouthed dog, so we all figured that had to be mine. After about an hour we heard them come around the ridge and the strange-mouthed dog that I thought was mine was in the lead. I was a little kid with three grown men, and I started giving them a hard time. I told them they needed a real dog like mine. About that time my dog came walking up to me and I saw that my dog hadn't even been in the hunt.

I grabbed up my dog and put an old rope around its neck. I think I ran the whole three miles home. I was ashamed of my dog and even more ashamed of how I had bragged in front of all those guys. That was when I learned that if you're going to brag about what you do, it's safer to do it after you've already done it rather than before you accomplish anything. Bragging before you start sets you up to find yourself in a bad situation.

When I met my wife—who was my girlfriend then—her dad had beagle dogs. He ran them in field trials, which are where they chase rabbits. They don't catch them, they just follow the scent. They don't even know what the rabbit looks like. Jo Ellen had told me about her daddy and how he had dogs, so I assumed we were going rabbit hunting. We got to her house late the first night and I still hadn't even met him. But I knew we were going hunting the next day and I wanted to impress him. The next morning he woke me up and he was already out back. I figured I better get ready to hunt, so I opened the trunk of my car and got my hunting coat and my shotgun and put some shells in. He walked up and said, "Oh, you won't need that, we don't use guns." I couldn't figure out what kind of crazy hunting we would be doing without guns. He handed me a stick and an orange for my lunch.

We went down there and chased rabbits all day, just running the dogs for the fun of it. I really liked it. We didn't shoot; we just enjoyed the dogs. Later he wanted me to go to a trial with him, where they run in competition. They judge which dog best follows the scent. I really liked the trials, too. That's how I got started. I got a few dogs and started breeding them.

If you win, you get some points, and if you get enough points, you get a national champion. I still enjoy it a lot. In our business, when you have a lot of building and development going and a lot of people working for you, you're affecting a lot of people's lives. It's not uncommon for there to always be some sort of a problem. Most days, around four or five in the afternoon, I take off and go with the dogs. Without having my dogs to get away from some of the pressure, I think I would've quit or gone crazy. That's not a joke, that's very serious. You have to be able to get away. Around the office, the phone rings and people want things. But when you're out there with the dogs, you're off by yourself and it's quiet. I've figured out more things about what I want to build and things like that outside with the dogs than anywhere else. It's quite a bit easier and certainly more peaceful than trying to figure that out in your office. You can't do anything at the office except answer the phone, try to get people to return your calls, and work.

I've met so many nice people working with the dogs. What makes it a great sport is that you don't have to join a club or have a car or anything like that. You just have to have a dog. You go meet people and run your dogs at a trial. They can be the richest person or poorest person in the

world and it doesn't make any difference. They just like dogs. Everybody has the same chance of having a good dog. Once in awhile, a person will come around and try to buy their way in, but it doesn't work. That really appeals to me. Just like everything else in life, you have to love what you're doing to be successful. You can do OK if you're just mildly interested in it, but you'll never be the best. A lot of people never learn that.

I refuse to win with a bought dog. Anybody with any money can buy a dog and win. I've never won with any dog that wasn't my dog, which means that I bred the mother and owned and raised the puppies. The fun is in breeding them and raising and training them. Then you can really win with your dog. I can't imagine that it would be very satisfying to go off and buy a dog and then win with it. You wouldn't have raised the dog, wouldn't have known where it came from. Trials are just a way to see the results of all the work you've put in with the dog when it was a puppy. It couldn't be very satisfying to get results when you didn't put in any work.

Chapter 2

Hauling Eggs to Building Lakes

When I was little, I always wanted to help the men do work. They'd give you the jobs that little people could do, but that didn't mean that you didn't have a job. You carried water and did other small things. If you didn't have any work to do, you still had an hour or hour and a half in the morning and afternoon of your regular work. For example, we had five or six cows that we milked every day by hand. Back then a company would send a truck around and we'd sell them class C milk, which was used to make cheese and a couple other products. We had a can that we'd set beside the road as a signal that we had some extra milk to sell.

In addition to the cows, we also had to feed the chickens and hogs, fork the hay, and other typical jobs that go along with living on a farm. Mountain people do that kind of thing every day, sometimes twice a day. That wasn't work, it was just part of life. Work was what you did after that. That's what you did every day, like eating. Or, to put it another way, if you wanted to eat, you did it.

When you'd hoe in the fields, you'd be so proud if you could outwork a man. It was such a big thing to try to hoe to the end of the row or pick up something better than a man could do. Today people seem to think that being competitive is a bad thing. I guess it might be if you always lose, but that's not the goal. We wanted to feel as though we were worth something. We'd just work and sweat, and we didn't even think we were working. We just thought it was a challenge and something to do. No matter how tired we were, we were so proud if we could do more than someone else.

The first time I remember outworking a man, I was probably about twelve or thirteen. We were putting a lot of hay up, which meant that we were cutting it in the field and when it got dry we'd put it up in the barn so that we could use it as feed in the winter. We had to put it on pitchforks, because we didn't have the machines and everything that they have now. I remember I couldn't hardly pick up as much as the men could on a pitchfork because it took all muscle and got real heavy when you had to pick it up and throw it way up on a stack. My physical strength wasn't as great as theirs, but my endurance was greater. I remember it was so hot. After you got sweating good, after about an hour or two, those old guys would start flaking out and I could do more than them, especially if it was hot. I learned then that if I persevered and worked hard, I'd eventually be successful. That's a valuable lesson to learn so early in life.

I remembered how important it had been to me to do work, and I tried to pass that on to my children. When my kids were eight or nine years old, they started working. Sometimes, they even worked together. When Andy, my oldest son, was between his first and second year in college, and Jeff, my youngest son, was eight or nine years old, they did some work for me. We were building a big lake over at Greystone, which is one of our developments. We were going to have a trail around the lake where people could walk or jog or fish. To be able to walk around the lake, though, we needed some bridges to get over the different tributaries that came into the lake.

I had been piling up old power company utility poles that the utility companies would throw away, because I thought we'd save some money and use those to make the bridges. We didn't want them to be fancy, but we didn't want them to take away from the quality of our development, either. Plus you had to be able to drive a tractor over them to keep it mowed and trimmed up neatly. I had an old Jeep with a pulley on it and thought Andy and Jeff could use that to pull those big old poles to make the bridge. Andy was studying civil engineering. I told him to take his little brother over there and build the bridges. They'd leave early in the morning, right around the time I got up. After about a day or so, they came back wanting to have a conference.

They said I didn't draw them a picture and they weren't sure how to build the bridges. I looked at Andy and said, "I'll tell you one thing. If I were a sophomore at N.C. State studying civil engineering and couldn't build a bridge across a creek no bigger than that, I wouldn't tell anybody." They went stomping out and slammed the door.

After that, they would come home at night and never mention the bridges. My wife kept asking me how they were doing and I told her I didn't know and that I wasn't going to insult them by going to look at it. That went on for maybe six weeks. One day, when I couldn't stand it anymore, I asked them about it. Jeff spoke up and said, "You're not interested, why are you asking? Just wait and see." So I could tell by the way he piped up they'd been talking about it a lot when they were out there on the job. It never came up again.

One day, about two or three o'clock in the afternoon, I heard that Jeep coming. They came walking in, smiling from ear to ear. They said they had finished the bridges and wanted me to come look at them. Well, those bridges might not have been exactly like I would've built them, but they were really pretty bridges. Jeff did most of the talking. I think his brother had told him what to say. He said, "Look, you don't see them bending or anything. These are strong bridges." They learned a lot doing that. They had to figure it out themselves. Everything that happened when it started, like me not showing them exactly how to do it, was worth twenty times that when I saw the pride on their faces. They accomplished something. Even today, they still tell people, "Yeah, we built the bridges over there, you know." Not many kids get an opportunity to do things like that. There's no better way to learn than to take the initiative and learn the joy of accomplishment.

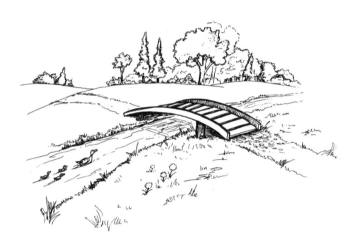

Jeff might have used some of what he learned later in life. He decided he was going to build houses. One night right after he had started he came over to our house. He said, "When I get the walls up, and I put the electric wires and plumbing and so forth in, then I'll put the drywall or the sheetrock up and cover up the wall. What happens if I didn't get something in the wall right? Then I'll have it covered up and won't be able to fix it." He really thought he was going to get a lot of help from me. I told him, "Hell, you tear it off and start all over and the next time you don't screw up." I think that's good advice.

His mother looked at him and said, "Well, he wasn't much help, was he?" I was probably more help than he thought. He built forty-seven houses in his first year, so yeah, he learned something.

It really gets me how many people are afraid to trust their kids or let them do things on their own. I'm sure it bothered my parents to let me do things that I did when I was little. It bothered me some when my kids started doing things. It's hard to turn them loose and trust them to do the right thing on their own. But that's what you have to do.

A few years ago, some people called me from a team of fourteen-year-old baseball players. They had made some type of playoffs and were going to Florida to play. They thought that instead of begging for money for nothing they would beg for money and act like they were doing some sort of service. Some of them decided to call me and see what they could do. I said I'd try to work with them. There were twelve or fourteen of them, and I had some land where people had dumped some trash. I told them I'd send a truck out there and they could load the truck and help clean up the place and I'd pay them minimum wage. They liked that idea, but a few days before they were supposed to come, a parent called to see if there were any briars on the property. I told him I wasn't sure. Then a daddy called wanting to know if there were any snakes out there. I told him I wasn't sure. Then another daddy called that worked for the EPA. He wanted to know if we had any hazardous waste out there and did we have any uniforms for them to wear.

By that point, it was starting to get ridiculous. As it turned out, they did nothing. The parents flat out gave them the money to go to Florida and the kids learned nothing except that they didn't have to work, they were chicken, and their parents were crazy. I didn't even really want them to come in the first place. They weren't going to

help me as much as I was going to pay them. They would
have at least gotten the satisfaction of working to earn their
trip out of the job, but they wound up not even getting that.
It's hard to believe that their parents would rather them
slack off and go to Florida for free instead of earning their
way. I guess some people just have a different idea of what
it takes to make it in this world.

My view was shaped by growing up on the farm. When
we weren't working on the farm, if we had any spare time,
we'd take the horses, tractor, or later on we had a truck and
my brothers and I would try to make money for ourselves.
We used to cut pulpwood a lot and haul it over to the
Champion Paper Company in Canton, which was about
forty miles away from where we lived. You could make
pretty good money, especially when you were boys, cutting
and selling pulpwood. We'd haul people's tobacco, bail
people's hay and all that stuff.

We always had to work hard, but Dad knew we wanted
extra money. He could have come up with more chores to
do or restricted us, but he always supported us trying to
make a little extra cash. When we had any spare time we
could do things to make money. When I was sixteen or
seventeen, I drove a school bus over big mountains. I drove
most of it on dirt roads. I barely even had my driver's
license and I'd be steering this big old bus around those
sharp mountain curves. I don't know what the parents of
the kids I was driving thought about it, but I thought it was
a good way to make money. That wasn't my only extra job,
though.

Mars Hill was a college town, and a lot of the professors
and administrators wanted to have gardens. They didn't
always know what they were doing, so I'd take a horse or
two and a plow and a disc and get them started. I'd break
up the dirt for the garden and prepare and smooth it. That
was the very first time that I learned not to work by the

hour. That was usually the first thing the college people would ask me: "How much per hour do you get paid?" They all figured that I was a little boy and wasn't going to work too fast. They didn't want to pay more than was necessary. They wanted to pay me little boy's wages. But if I got a flat rate for each job, I could work faster and do more in one day, which meant I got paid more.

One time when I was out on a job, I had forgotten some of my equipment, so I left my horse tied to an apple tree and walked about a mile and a half back to my house to get my plow. The guy I was working for was this big old guy. While I was gone, he untied my horse and hooked it up to the disc and jumped up and down on the disc. I wasn't there, so I had no idea that he had pushed the disc even further into the ground, which made it more difficult for the horse to pull. When I got back he was standing up on that disc, making the horse go even faster. I guess he thought he was going to get the job for free by using my tools and my horse. My horse was really sweating and I didn't like to see my horse sweat. I also didn't like people thinking they could do whatever they wanted with my tools.

I packed up my stuff and went home when I figured out what he had done. He came to see my dad thinking he was going to get me in trouble, but my dad agreed with me. He said if I went back there that the man should leave me alone and let me do my work. Needless to say, it didn't make that man overly happy that a little boy and his father were telling him that he had been in the wrong. But no matter how old you are, people should have to treat you right. Just because you're smaller than them doesn't mean that you're incompetent.

My uncle had an egg business in Asheville and he had some trucks he used to haul eggs. Back then, North Carolina imported about ninety percent of all its eggs. My daddy worked with him some and my brothers and I also helped occasionally. He'd go up to Indiana and Illinois and pick up the eggs and bring them back. We'd grade the eggs and then sell them. He had a contract with Biltmore Farms, Swift and Company, and other businesses like that. Once we got the eggs back from up North, our job was to put the eggs in cartons that had the names of each business on them.

One of the customers we delivered eggs to was the Grove Park Inn, a big fancy hotel in Asheville. It was a big deal back then and an even bigger deal now. People always think they're real fancy if they get to go to Asheville and stay at the Grove Park. I used to take eggs there for a long time and I'd look at those people checking in and think about how rich they must be. Several years ago, some friends invited us up there to spend some time. I drove up to register and I found out I was at the back door, because I was where I used to deliver eggs. We were supposed to go to the front door, where the guests entered. I didn't know any better. I was just going to the place that I was used to going.

Anyway, my uncle always needed somebody to drive the trucks. When I was fourteen or fifteen, my brother would drive the trucks, since he was two or three years older than me. I'd ride with him and then drive at night because there weren't many cops on the road. It wasn't a good idea for me to drive during the day, because I didn't have my license. This was before they had interstates and all the big roads. One time we were up in Indiana early in the morning and my brother fell asleep while I was driving. They used to put mailboxes in a line, six or eight together in a bunch. I drove off the edge of the road and knocked down a whole line of mailboxes. My brother decided he'd be honest and call the cops. They took his license because he told them that he was the one that knocked down the mailboxes, even though I had been the one driving.

I started driving on the farm when I was ten or eleven. The day I turned sixteen, August 27th, I went to the driver's license bureau, took the test, and received my first driver's license. I was the first one there, because I couldn't wait. At 10:30 that morning I left in a truck to get a load of eggs. I had my license so there wasn't any sense in waiting. I was ready to get to work right that minute.

I guess a lot of people think I've made my boys grow up too fast by letting them do dangerous work so young. I remember Jeff a few years ago worked seventy-two hours a week for a grading contractor running all kinds of heavy equipment. When he worked over forty-eight hours he'd get paid time-and-a-half, and then eventually was paid double time. When he got the check that summer, he had enough to go to school for almost an entire year. He might not have thought all that work was worth it at the time, but I bet he did once he realized he could use it for a whole year of school. You can't protect your kids; you let them grow up. I still believe that so much. My kids learned to work early, just like I did. When I got my driver's license, I was ready to do work that day.

Another time I went to Chicago to get the eggs. I was sixteen or seventeen and had a big old truck. I loved to go to the truck stops because all the girls thought I was a little boy. They'd be all nice to me and give me something to eat. After you got your eggs loaded, you had to stop somewhere and call back to the office to tell them you were loaded and coming back. We even developed a system where I would call collect and they wouldn't take the call, but they would still know where I was. The truck was loaded so I called and they said, "Man, we've been looking for you everywhere. Don't go, don't go."

I said, "Well, I've already loaded my eggs, what's wrong?"

They said, "They're on strike up there, the whole waterfront's on strike, you don't go when they're on strike in Chicago."

I said, "Well, I did notice some guys standing down there in the road and I just kind of drove around them. And then nobody helped me load the eggs so I just loaded my own. I figured maybe up there people don't work on Saturday." I didn't know what a union or a strike was. I just went and got my eggs.

Another time, my cousin drove up there for the eggs. He was about nineteen or twenty, a little older than me. They loaded his eggs real early on a Sunday morning. He pulled up to a stoplight on the edge of town and two guys jumped up on the running boards and surprised him. They had a gun and told him to lie down. They covered him up with an old quilt that was in the truck. They took the truck back to the egg place, unloaded the eggs, and then drove back to where they had jumped him.

He was right back where he had started, but it was four hours later and he didn't have the eggs. They held him at the police station for five hours thinking he had stolen the eggs. I'm almost sure that the police were in cahoots with those guys. One time after that, I was back up there and they had stolen the little trolley-type thing you roll the eggs on. The serial number on the trolley they were using at the egg place was the same one that had been on our truck when it was hijacked. That was one of the first times I ever learned about how cops operated in the big city.

I guess that incident was my first experience with insurance companies. It really shaped the way that I deal with them now and my opinions about them. I think that if you don't have to have it, the best insurance is no insurance. You never know if you have the right kind of insurance to cover what you have. For example, we had theft insurance on those eggs. We figured, "Well, we've got insurance, so we'll get money back." After all, that's why we had been paying the insurance. Nope. The truck was in motion, so they called that hijacking. They didn't tell us that when we got the insurance, but now it turned out that our insurance didn't apply. To cover that, we would've had to have hijacking insurance. I guess they thought you could just walk down and get it at the drugstore in Asheville or something.

For a short period of time later on, I actually worked for an insurance company. I learned one thing. They have one floor divided up between sales, marketing, and every other department you can imagine. Then there's one whole floor made up of legal people making sure they don't have to pay out any money for claims. The legal people take up twice as much room as all the other departments.

I try never to buy insurance unless it's a requirement and I can't get around it. I don't believe in carrying collision insurance on cars or anything like that. When you buy insurance, first the company keeps at least forty percent. If you pay them $100 and then they have to pay out $60, they're ready to cancel your insurance. You just threw $40 down a rat hole. Most people would scoff at $40 and say it's not that much, but it adds up when you think about it.

It's the same way with health insurance. Now we've got HMOs, PPOs, and all kinds of things that have abbreviations that I don't even know what they mean. The bottom line is somebody found doctors—the people that used to be the bastion of free enterprise—and got them on a contract. The man in charge of one of the biggest HMOs made around $32 million last year. That's pretty good work if you can get it. I don't think the system we have now will ever work until we cut out the middleman and make the customer go straight to the doctor. Then, all the benefits come straight back to the customer. Then, people would have a personal interest in taking care of themselves. They'd pay attention to how often they went to the doctor and how much they spent. If people are given health insurance, there's no incentive to spend as little as possible.

I think it's important to teach kids to be self-sufficient early on. I don't ever remember asking one of my kids if they had done their homework. It never came up. They knew to do it. I would have considered it an insult to even ask them. They knew not to come in with any bad grades, because they knew what we expected. I don't ever remember even having to wake one up to go to school or work. They could set an alarm clock just as well as I could. They knew they could either get up and get out the door or they could stay in the bed and get their butt beaten. It was their choice.

I think they appreciated what I told them because they knew I had lived that way. They had heard me talk about the odd jobs I had when I was growing up, and they knew that if I could do it, they could do it.

When I was only in the third or fourth grade, I went to the livestock market in Asheville with my dad, where they bought and sold cows and just about anything else. It was an auction market. It was always interesting to see how much things would bring. One day there were two goats, a mother goat and a baby goat. I saw them and really wanted them. I had my hand up trying to get my dad's attention and the auctioneer thought I was bidding. He said, "Sold! To this little man back there!" I remember it cost me $2.75. They were just glad to get rid of them, because no one wanted them.

We didn't have the truck with us and we had also bought a few cows. We had to go back up there the next day to pick them up. When we got there, we couldn't find them and I was just about crying. The man said, "Those dang goats chewed up everything we've got. They even chewed the rope and let the cows out. You go get them out of that little shack over there and I don't want to see them again."

I took them home and a few days after that, a man stopped by wanting to know if I would sell goat's milk. He lived right over by the school, so I made a deal that every morning I'd take him one quart of milk. Since I rode the school bus, I carried a quart of milk with me every morning on the bus and left it on his porch. He paid $.80 per quart and paid me once a week. I thought I was rich. I had paid $2.75 for the goats and now I was making $.80 per quart for their milk. Once again, I was learning about how to make a profit.

That wasn't the only way that we made some extra money. Down below the house, a mile or two away, was a place where two streams came together. During rains, a lot of sand would settle there. My brother and I would sell the sand and make blocks. We'd take a horse or two in the summertime and drag a pan behind the horses in the water. That would allow us to create a big pile of sand up on the bank. If anyone came along and wanted to buy sand, we'd just load it on a truck by shovel. Now, if you get someone that needs even a small amount, like one-fourth of a load or something, they want to get a truck and dump it. They don't ever think about doing it by hand. They want to go get a truck loader and lots of equipment.

We also had a deal where we made concrete blocks. We had four forms. We could make three blocks in each form at one time. We had a mixing box and we'd use the shovel to put sand and a little concrete in there. Then, we'd take a bucket and some water and work it back and forth with a hoe until we had mixed concrete. We'd fill forms with concrete and then set them out to dry. When you knocked the forms off, they would have gotten hard and you'd have a block. That's how people got blocks to build with. We made the ones that we used to build the septic tank when we put the bathroom in the house.

Even at that, though, I didn't feel like I was getting along fast enough, so I rented some land from another fellow. Usually, when you rented land you had to give the other guy half and you got half. But this guy had some land that was grown up with briars, probably five or six acres of it. I made a deal with him that I'd get two-thirds of what grew on it. I figured that was a better deal even though it was a harder place to work. All I had to do was clear a few briars and I'd make more money than I would on regular land. I was going to raise corn, and I did.

I started gathering that corn. I had a wagon and two horses to pull the wagon. I'd get a wagonload and take it to him, and then I'd get two wagonloads and take it to me. I was dividing it up two-thirds and one-third, just like our agreement. Just when I was going good he came and said, "No, man, you're cheating me." He told me I had to get all that corn back and put it in three piles and he'd pick out which pile he wanted. I figured that meant I'd have to load it and unload it twice, but that's what I did. I had to, because that's what he said would make him happy. We finally got the deal worked out and I had lots of good quality corn.

After that, I was going to raise me some pigs and sell them myself. We'd always raised pigs when I was little and I used to sell some when they were small. The buyer would feed them and eventually slaughter them for meat. I'd put the babies in a sack and when they were big enough to sell, about six weeks old, I'd walk a mile or two around and some of the neighbors would buy them.

I needed more pigs than I had, though, so I figured my best bet was to buy some pigs to feed the corn that I would grow on my land. Down in the country, peddlers used to come buy chickens or eggs or to sell other things. Some had an old car or truck. Peddlers would come around selling about everything. One day a guy came around selling pigs. He was from Tennessee, about thirty miles away from where we lived, and he probably had ten or twenty pigs. I got on his truck and looked those pigs over. They had curly hair and a curly tail, and looked really nice to me. They were slightly bigger than little pigs and must've weighed forty pounds. I thought they were a real buy. I believe they were $8 or $10 apiece. I had enough money saved up to buy them, so I did. I thought I was on the verge of starting my master plan. I had the corn to feed the pigs and now I had the pigs to go with it.

After awhile my daddy got home. He looked at those pigs and said, "God knows, the reason those pigs have curly hair, they're those ol' Tennessee pigs. They've got screwworms and they're stunted. You can feed them all the corn you've got and they're not going to grow very fast. You really got took." I got all upset. I wanted to go find that guy and make him give me my money back. My dad said,

"No, you looked at them before you bought them. You're the one that did that." It doesn't sound like much, but I learned very early on to be responsible for whatever I did. That's why I don't have much patience these days when people try to weasel their way out of accepting responsibility for what they do. Very rarely is it accurate to say that anything is totally not your fault. If people would spend the same amount of time in the first place to do things right that they do trying to deny it was their fault, most everything would be done correctly the first time.

When I used to sell my pigs and corn and other stuff, it was an open market. If you wanted to buy it, you bought it. If not, you didn't. That's what I grew up with and was used to. I didn't know anything else happened. It seemed to make perfect sense to me. If the price was too high, you didn't pay. If you wanted to grow more and make more money, then you did.

Then they came along with a tobacco program, which meant that a person was given an allotment, and he was only allowed to grow so many acres of tobacco. When I was in high school, I decided I wanted a good job, so I'd go measure tobacco acreage. I'd measure it and I'd have to tell a man that he couldn't have any more than I measured. If he had more, it had to go. Even further up in the mountains than where I was from, people were a little more independent. They told me they didn't like people measuring their tobacco and telling them what they could grow because they were used to doing what they wanted to.

If I went up there and figured they had too much, I was to stand there and watch them cut it down. They weren't too fond of the government up there, and when some young boy came and said he was going to stand there while they cut their tobacco down, they didn't get the hang of that. It wasn't the open market that they were used to or that I was used to, for that matter.

Now we've got the cigarette program. By charging a larger tax per pack of cigarettes, people who can't afford to pay more money are charged more and that money goes to the government. Now Clinton wants the federal government to go back and get even more money. Now all the governors are in on it and getting money from the tobacco companies. They're having a field day playing Santa Claus with someone else's money. I hope I didn't help start that plan when I was cutting down that guy's tobacco.

We've decided that smoking is bad for your health. We also decided that growing tobacco is good for the economy. Well, you can't have it both ways. We've told the companies they have to charge more money for cigarettes so they can make more money to give to the government. The farmer has to get the money so he can make his payments on the equipment that enables him to keep growing tobacco. I don't understand the logic in that. People say nicotine is addictive. So is telling people you'll guarantee them a price whether they grow a crop or not.

Somehow, we've decided that tobacco is worse than alcohol. The cigarette companies aren't allowed to use Joe Camel, but Budweiser can show those stupid frog commercials during every basketball and football game in the world. Every kid growing up in this area watches those games. All they see on commercials are people drinking beer and having fun. How is a cartoon camel more harmful to kids than cartoon frogs? Every time you turn on the television, you see quarterback John Elway sitting in front of a bunch of pretty mountains and drinking a Coors beer. As much influence as athletes have, you think that doesn't appeal to kids?

Smoking cigarettes may be bad for a person's health, but it doesn't harm anyone else. Alcohol can kill innocent people. When I taught Sunday school, one of our students was involved in a drunk driving accident. People were killed because he chose to drink alcohol and get behind the wheel of a car. My wife and I went to court and served as character witnesses for him. It was terrible to see the families of the people that were killed. Their whole lives had been changed by someone else's choices. All I could think while we sat there and listened to the terrible things they had been through was, "Well, at least he wasn't smoking a cigarette."

• • •

One time a man up in the mountains had a cow that went crazy. The cow was mean and people were afraid to get close to her. So the word went out that whoever could catch her would get what she was worth. That didn't sound like much work to me, so I figured I would catch her.

I talked to my daddy about the best way to do it. He said he was sure she was hungry. We had a tobacco barn that hadn't been used in awhile. I made a heavy door for the front of the barn. I put out some food. The next day, I put out a little more food. I'd see the cow around, but she'd always be gone by the time I got there. I eventually worked my way up to putting some food inside the barn. I walked down there and the cow was inside the barn eating the food that I had left. I knew I'd not have time to get close enough to shut the door before the cow got out without spooking her and then she might not come back.

I had done a little trapping in my life and caught a few muskrats, beavers, and other things. I fixed a latch on that door and tied a string to it. Then I ran the string 150 yards or so up in the woods. Finally, after four or five days, the cow got to where she really liked it in that barn. She'd hang around for a little while. She came to depend on that barn for something to eat and she let her guard down. I slammed that door with my rope and sold that cow.

The moral of the story is: If you let people start baiting you, you'll bite off a little more, and then a little more, and then a little more. Pretty soon, they've got you. That's what happens to people. If you don't believe it, look at Social Security, Medicaid, welfare, and other government programs. People usually don't even know they're acting that way. You can get so dependent that they'll do what you tell them without even realizing it. We've even reached the point where people will vote for a womanizing draft dodger if they think he'll give them something. Clinton might as well give everyone that voted for him five dollars, since it's so much like buying votes.

Nowadays it seems like everyone likes to blame everyone else. My daughter was at school one time and they said to go buy the cheapest house you could get and then go to the government and make the inspectors get the builder to redo it correctly. I thought you were supposed to check around and see who builds good houses and then buy from them. Wouldn't you rather have a house that was built right the first time by a good builder than a cheap house done by a builder that couldn't get it right?

If my parents didn't do anything else, they taught us to be one hundred percent responsible for whatever we did. You went and looked in the mirror, not somewhere else. If you got in trouble at school, you got your butt beat when you got home and then after that they talked to you about what happened. They weren't going to start asking about whose fault it was. If you got in trouble, it was your fault. Now any time that something bad happens, we've got to call in the lawyers and have them analyze everything to determine who was at fault. Why don't you just ask the people that were involved and let them tell you?

I learned about responsibility at church, too. I remember one time in high school or late junior high, me and about five or six other boys my age thought we were such a big deal for running off our Sunday school teachers. We wouldn't be quiet, no matter what they said. We were proud of the fact that two or three left, and one of them had cried. Then, we got a new Sunday school teacher—a big guy from Mars Hill College named John Brown. He was a veteran. There were a lot of veterans around in the late '40s. He came in and he said, "OK, now you boys get out of here and leave, we're not going to have Sunday school today. When you come back next Sunday you're mine. No more of your crazy acting up starting next week."

We thought, "Yeah, we've heard that before." We left and came back the next Sunday. He moved our class from our Sunday school room to the baptistery, which was filled with water when people were being baptized. The rest of the time it was empty and you could sit in it. It was small. I guess it was a six or eight foot square, so it was real crowded in there, and he could reach every one of us. We started class and one of the guys said something. Then I started a little bit of foolishness. Well, John Brown cracked me on the top of the head so hard I thought he had busted it. That got my attention good and after that we were real quiet in there. He was different from the other teachers we had in the past because he hadn't just said he was going to do something about us acting up. He had actually done it.

We eventually started liking him. He played center field on the baseball team. He came by my house and brought me his baseball glove when he left after teaching our class for two years. We had gone from him thumping me on the head to bringing me his baseball glove. That's quite a transition.

Kids like to be kept straight. They like to be made to do what's right. Now it seems like we don't believe that. I know what worked for us. It straightened my mess out in a hurry. It's so important to learn individual responsibility, to take blame for what you do and suffer the consequences. We've gotten so far from that now it's pitiful.

My son David has been very active in the church. One time, they were discussing raising kids. He's got a little girl. They were talking about if so-and-so, what do you do, and if this-and-that, what do you do. Are you supposed to set the example, use cause and effect, or what? They were talking about drugs and alcohol and they asked David, "If you had come home with drugs or alcohol, what would your dad have done to you?"

David's reply was, "You mean after I got up off the ground?" That's not a bad way to be, but we sure don't have a lot of it right now.

Every one of my kids started working forty hours a week when they were eight or nine years old while they were out of school for the summer. They'd go to church camp or sports camp for a week or two. It was like a big ceremony that every summer they would have to come in to tell me how much time they were planning to take for vacation and how much of their earnings they were planning on putting in their savings account.

When they first started working, we'd start them with whatever they could do. My daughter would go with my wife and wash windows, clean the carpet, get the inside of the houses clean, and all those things. My sons started off riding bicycles to the job sites. They'd help with the trash truck, picking up the yards, and they would work their way up. They'd save their money and put it in the bank.

I worked my way through the early part of my life and I learned more through that than I did going to school. Every one of my children knew I'd done that. My oldest son, Andy, was the first of our bunch to go to college. I don't even remember discussing the money with him. He just applied, was accepted, and went. He worked his way through school. I didn't give any of the rest of them help with their school either. I didn't help them directly, other than with jobs in the summer and in other ways to make sure they had a job.

They saved their own money. Jeff called on the phone one time from Carroll Junior High and wanted his mother to get on the phone. He was in the sixth grade and had paid for something with a check. The lady had said a kid couldn't write a check, so she wouldn't take it. My kids had their own bank accounts and wrote checks from the time they were eight or nine years old. It was their money and they learned if they spent it they didn't have any more. It didn't come from the sky. When it was gone, it was gone. If they put more money there, at the end of the year the bank would add interest on, and that was like magic. That was like money from heaven or something. That's an important lesson to learn.

David went to Wake Forest, which cost more than N.C. State or Chapel Hill, where the government foots most of the bill. He called one time and said, "I've got to make big money if I'm going to pay this tuition bill. I'm not making enough working at construction jobs over the summer." This was after his first year at Wake. He called around and a guy gave him a name of someone in Texas to call. Through that contact, he got a job working oil rigs in Texas that paid two to three times what he was making around here.

His mother worried sick about him when he left. The first time he called he was at a Laundromat. He was still looking for a place to spend the night but he was washing his clothes. We figured that was one out of two, which isn't bad. There wasn't a soul around that spoke English. Everybody spoke Spanish or something crazy like that.

In the next day or two, he went to church and met the pastor's son who was home for the summer. They had a place out behind their house and that boy invited him to stay with him for the summer. You can call that luck or whatever you want to, but it wasn't luck that someone taught him to go to church.

He made a bunch more money that summer than he had been making at home. He wound up quitting a week or two before the summer was over, because they were laying off people since the oil business was going down a little bit. They came in to lay off four guys. They told David he worked so well that they weren't going to lay him off. They hoped he might even come back and work for them after college. But they were laying off two other guys who had families and David had seen their wives around there with little kids. He quit so that they wouldn't lose their jobs.

I'm very proud that all our children are risk-takers. Andy just announced a project in Wake Forest and they had an article about it in the paper. They said it might be a $500 million project with all the land he's doing. You can't make any bigger headlines than he did in the paper that day, and they even said nice things about him, which is rare for the news media.

Alma has her own business, too. She writes books and teaching aids for teachers. She also puts on seminars and training programs for teachers to upgrade their certificates and learn new techniques. She does a lot of camps and has started Camp Invention in this area, which are summer camps that teach kids the thrill of making and inventing things. I'm very proud of what she's done. Her husband, John, also has his own business.

What makes me proudest is that they haven't decided that just because we've made a dollar they want to get their hands on it or spend it or anything else. They want to take a risk just like we've always done. They even quote me now, because they've heard me say so many times, "I know I can live with being broke, but I can't live with thinking I was being a chicken."

One of the things I enjoy most about working is that my whole family has been involved. My wife always helped make a project work so we could pay off the bank and try to get some extra money. We've spent our life doing that. One time she said she wasn't sure she wanted it to work, because she knew that if we made $10, all we'd do is go borrow $90 more to go with it and start buying something else and taking more risks. She said it's just been one big roller coaster for her. Every time I tell her this might be the last time, that's never true. She really is caught up in it like the rest of us. Jo Ellen had to help us with the business and raise four kids at the same time. One time, I remember her telling me she didn't think we had enough money to make it. I told her that I knew how hard she had tried to make ends meet and I would just have to make more. It gave her confidence that we were levelheaded about money.

I've always liked to take chances, even in my life outside of work. I like to go to car races, so one time I decided to go to Buck Baker's Driving School. I figured it was only driving a car, so it shouldn't be too hard. My wife gave Andy and me a deal where we could go to the driving school for four days down at Rockingham Speedway. We got to drive the cars around the track and everything. I don't ever remember enjoying anything so much in my life. The cars were built so well. I wasn't real good at going so fast and having cars driving only six feet in front of me.

One time we were practicing drafting. We were going into a curve. At this time, Andy had a beard, and he was right behind me. I glanced up at the stand and Buck Baker was up there motioning for us to get closer together. When I looked in the mirror Andy was so close that all I could see was a helmet and a beard. You couldn't even see the hood of his car. I was doing 150 miles an hour and I was wondering if he knew I was going to slow down up there in that corner.

A lot of my friends always say they want to be involved in investments and risk-taking, making more than they do in a standard account with an interest rate of five or six percent. But when it gets to nut-cutting time, which is what I call it when it's time to sign your name on the line as being personally responsible and risk losing your house or car, they seem to change their mind. They want to know what assurance they have that they aren't going to lose their money. You tell them there's absolutely no assurance. After that they don't want to be a risk-taker like they thought they wanted to be. It's funny how that turns out.

All my kids worked their way through school and did well, not because they had to, but because they wanted to. The "wanting to" is a lot more important than the "having to." It seems like the first thing the government does now if someone needs something is make other people do something for them instead of making them figure out how to help themselves.

When you hand stuff to people, they get used to it. The minute the handout is gone, they still don't know how to help themselves and you're right back where you started.

They don't instill any initiative in their kids, so nothing carries on. You don't get any good out of the handout. The greatest disservice done to our country has been all the giveaways and handout programs, like Social Security and welfare that Franklin Roosevelt started. They began that right around my birthday on August 27, 1935.

When Social Security started, people only had to pay one or two percent of their salary. It was set up so that people would get back their own money that they had paid in when they were working. It was going to be kind of like a parachute—something to help out if all else failed. That doesn't sound like such a bad idea when you put it that way.

But now, the money comes from other workers and the individual and their employer have to pay fourteen percent. People think that since they only have to pay half of that, it's OK, but they're really paying it all. If I didn't have to pay taxes on my employees, I could give that money straight to them. Workers also think they're getting a break because if they get a second job, they'll get that money back, but the employer's share doesn't come back. Now the trend is to cap the maximum that you can get. If you don't need it, you don't get it. It was going to be kind of like a parachute that would help you if everything else went bad. Now we've made it into something it was never supposed to be.

Over half of all Americans pay more in Social Security than they do in income tax. We pay it out to so many who don't work to get it, that those who are working have to work harder to pay more. The ratio of Social Security recipients to workers is about 3.3-to-1 right now. In twenty years or so, it'll be down to 2-to-1. As that continues to go down, it doesn't sound as though those workers have much of a future, does it?

Currently, it takes over twenty years after retirement to recoup what you paid in to Social Security when you were working, if you're fortunate enough to live that long. By 2005, it's going to take thirty years. In the 1980s, it took four years.

My accountants figured up how much I have paid into Social Security. Since I have several companies, I pay my share several times. If I had invested everything I paid at four to six percent, I would have received many times what I will ever get. What little I do get from Social Security will be taxed at over fifty percent. It doesn't take a smart man to realize that that's a bad deal. We've turned what started to be a nice little thing to help people over the hump into a welfare program.

One thing you can say about our government: they can take something that was started for a good reason and just let it keep on rolling whether it works or not. Once they start something, it's like a freight train. I don't know where Social Security will end. Pretty soon people will have to retire at the age of twenty-eight if they want to get back all the money they paid in Social Security. People aren't going to stand for the workers paying for the non-workers forever. As long as people get elected by giving money to people who don't work, the chance of stopping them is not too good. Maybe a good idea would be getting Mrs. Clinton to handle the investment of that money just like she did with her own money in the futures market. If we could multiply it by one hundred times in a short time like she did, the country might make it after all.

It's like the story about the little boy who wanted to buy a bicycle. The bicycle was going to cost him $100. He couldn't decide how in the world he was going to be able to afford it. He thought maybe he could raise the money and he'd start by writing a letter to God. So he did, and told him he could sure use $100 to buy the bicycle, and if there were any way that God could help, that would be great.

Well, of course the post office didn't know what to do with the letter, so they figured they would send it to the President in Washington. The President thought he would try to be nice, so he told one of his advisors to send the boy $5. When the boy got the letter, he noticed it was postmarked in Washington. He got the $5 and wrote God back, "Thank you very much for the money you sent to help me buy the bicycle. But I'm sorry you had to send it through Washington because those jerks took $95 of the $100 that you sent me."

Another great disservice was the civil rights movement in the 1960s. Now, I know that's not politically correct. I know that people are probably rolling their eyes right now. But what I think about it doesn't have anything to do with the skin color of the people involved. It has to do with the attitude that was instilled in people. I am sure that a lot of people meant well and thought it was a good idea, but it sure put an attitude into people of deserving and wanting rights instead of wanting to work to get ahead and do good.

This is when we coined the word "entitlement," which means people feel like they're owed something. I've never understood people that feel like they deserve something for no good reason. In the time it takes to organize a protest march, all those people could be out on the job site working their way up in the world. But the problem was that it made people think they deserved to start right at the top without having to work up or that they have the right to things without working for them. That's not how it is in the real world, but that attitude still prevails so much.

If anybody would look around and open their eyes and see what we see on the job, they'd understand what is happening. I'm not sure if we'd be in the construction business if it weren't for Mexicans. Once again, it's got nothing to do with their skin color. It has to do with their attitude towards work. Other people just don't want to work anymore. If we tell a Mexican we need three more workers in the morning, I guarantee you there will be three more. I've never known one that didn't want to work, work hard, and was happy about working. They don't even speak the language and they can understand what you want better than a lot of people that speak English.

When Hurricane Fran came through North Carolina in 1996, there were trees everywhere. My daughter had eight of them on her house. We decided we were going to marshal up twenty-five or thirty men for an emergency crew. We were asking around where to get them, and we asked one of the young guys that worked for us if there was anyone in his town that might want a job. He told us that there were lots of them, but they weren't planning on working. I guess they were standing around waiting for someone to hand them something. We told one Mexican and he told some of his friends and within three days we had filled out our crew.

I don't want to make myself sound like a hero or something, because that's not what I was. I just never assumed that anything would happen unless I wanted it to happen and worked to get it. My parents helped me learn that there were ways to make things happen for good and to be successful. I read a quote one time that was so true: "Knowing where you want to be in the end is better than a detailed plan. Dreaming and soaring is more exhilarating than going one step at a time."

Chapter 3
Marching for Free

All my life it was important to me to get an education. People will say to me, "Well, you grew up in the mountains," and you can tell that they think you were poor and uneducated. I had friends that went to Duke and places like that. When they found out I was from the mountains, they assumed we intermarried and all had big heads. We never thought of ourselves that way. We thought we had it made, to tell you the truth.

It wasn't like we never thought about education. Generations before me, around 1865 or 1866, the time the Civil War was over, the ancestor that I'm named after had been a missionary for the Baptist Association up in the mountains. There was nowhere for people to go to school after the eighth or ninth grade up there, so he helped start a little school in Mars Hill. That grew into what is now Mars Hill College, a Baptist college. My family had a lot to do with that and I had a couple ancestors that helped get the school started. One of them was one of the first presidents of the college.

Everybody took education real seriously. I don't believe since then there's been anyone in the Ammons family that didn't go to college and I don't know many families that can say that. If you didn't have but so much money, no matter what you had, you took it very seriously that you were going to school and you were going to do well.

I just love mechanical things and fixing them. I like physics, trigonometry, algebra, and all those subjects. The biggest change that's come about in the past few years, and I guess it's made me obsolete, is that we've substituted electronics for mechanical things. We used to have pulleys or cogs but now we have electronics.

When hay-balers first came out, they were designed to tie up the hay, first with wire and later with string. Hay-balers had knotters, which was the part of the machine that, when you got enough hay, would cut it off and tie a knot and get ready to tie another one. It was real complicated and hard to fix. I wasn't even old enough to drive when I learned how to fix them. I fixed them for quite a few people in the area. It seems like a little thing when I think about it now, but that was the beginning of when I knew I wanted to work with machines.

When I was deciding to go to college, I knew I wanted to study something mechanical. I liked farming and wanted to make farming life easier, so I decided to study agricultural engineering. At the time, Clemson had the reputation as one of the best agricultural engineering schools in the country. I had made up my mind I probably wanted to go there. All my family went to Mars Hill, but I decided I didn't want to go that close to home.

It's funny, because now I'm a trustee at Mars Hill, helping to continue what my ancestor began. I've heard a lot of stories about all the hard times they had getting the school started, things like selling a slave to keep the college going. It has quite a history and I still have a lot of interest in it. Then, though, I didn't have the least bit of interest in going there myself. Mars Hill has become very important to me. Although I didn't go there for college, it has played a major role in my later life.

I knew my parents loved Mars Hill College more than anything in the world. Being a trustee, I always thought about what I might do to have some impact. We decided that, since the baby boomers are coming of age, one of the trends of the future will be care for the elderly. After all, people have to live a long time if they're going to get back any of that Social Security that they paid! That's how our interest in retirement living and nursing homes came about.

We decided that one of the ways to help the college was to build an assisted-living elderly retirement facility on the campus to not only attract more attention to the area, but to help many of the people in the area. We wanted to build a good assisted-living facility around Mars Hill, something of which we could all be proud. We're building one, and we hope it will have some positive impact on the college and help a lot of people.

We've been working on it now for about a year. It takes a lot of time to get everything through the government. We have to meet with someone who has never built a facility like this, never changed a sheet, never risked his money to help a person, nothing like that. No matter how good you want to do it or how good you've done it before, you still have to get permission from somebody. We messed with them for over one year, but we finally started and will be open before this book is printed.

We hope we'll be able to help the area a little bit, because private colleges are having a hard time keeping the doors open. There are a few big ones, like Duke or Harvard, which are different. The mainstream ones are having it very tough right now.

One of the big responsibilities as a trustee is raising money. To raise money, you've got to go to somebody who has money. It's like Al Capone said when they asked him why he robbed banks: "That's where the money is." If you're going to raise money, you've got to go where the money is. A lot of our time is spent doing that. You say you have tuition of $10,000 or $12,000 a year, but most students aren't willing to pay that because they can go to a state school and pay much less. To me, it seems the state schools, which are run by taxpayers' money, are trying to put the private colleges out of business. Anybody who doesn't believe that is not a realist. If you're going to keep a private school open, you've got to go to the people with money, and they're the ones paying the taxes. So, you might be the highest taxpayer in the highest bracket, and here we are asking you to give money to a private college.

You've got to make enough money for the government to take most of it and be your competition and then give more to another school to keep them from going broke because you paid for their competition. If that's not a circle, I don't know what one is.

The state now says they pay for people to go to private colleges. I think it's $2,000 a year or so now. The state probably pays $9,000 or $10,000 for a student to go to N.C. State, UNC, or other state-supported schools, and that doesn't include the buildings, which they pay for separately. It's either got to be because they consider it good business, or because they think state schools give a better education, or they want to control what people learn. And they say, "We're not controlling what people do." They'll say, "Jud, we'll pay for you to go to NCSU, but if you go to Wake Forest, you have to pay your own way." That's not controlling? Well, State's playing East Carolina in football, aren't they? You think they wanted to play them? The legislature did that, so saying they don't have control isn't right.

One time I ran for the Board of Governors for the UNC system and had a question-and-answer session with some of the legislators. One asked me, "Mr. Ammons, if you were on the board and something came up and you didn't agree with us, what would you do?"

"Well, what do you think I'd do?" I said. "I'd do what I thought I was supposed to do."

"You wouldn't do what we told you?"

I said, "Shucks no. If you want to do that you go be on the board yourself."

Needless to say, I didn't get on the board. To say that they don't want to have control is wrong. What they ought to do is give you more like $7,000 if you want to go to a private school instead of a state school, and they'd still be saving money. Then the private schools wouldn't constantly have to be begging for money. People are saying now that you are getting a better education at a state school, but I doubt that. They act like they're proud of it and there's no reason for that. They ought to be giving a whole lot better education, because they've got all the money they want, and other people are begging. I can't see where students no longer having a choice serves the public interest. The cost is basically making the choice for most of them right now. If one is $10,000 and one is $2,000 and you don't have any money, then you don't have any choices.

People want to make the case that the government giving money to private colleges defies the Constitution by violating the separation of church and state. They wouldn't be giving the money to the school, but to an individual who could then make a personal choice. The truth is that doing things that way wouldn't defy the separation of church and state more than the state trying to put private colleges out of business.

Anyway, I was too young to realize any of this when I was choosing where to go to college. I saved up a little bit of money and signed up to go to Clemson, which was about two or three hours from where I grew up. It was a lot closer than N.C. State was, which was in Raleigh and was a long ways from the mountains. I went down to South Carolina to check it out. When I got there, the students were all marching around and around. I said, "What are those dudes doing?" They told me Clemson was a military school. If you remember, Clemson was a military school right up until 1955 or so. I decided right then that I wasn't going to pay to march. That was ridiculous. I could march at home for free. I didn't want to do that crap. I came back and got into State. Within a day or two I was on my way to Raleigh.

I had several hundred dollars saved up when I left home for college. It was money I had saved from cutting pulpwood, selling my pigs, all the little jobs that I had done. It wasn't like I had been out wasting it on a bunch of silly stuff. When it came time to go to school, I caught a ride with a fellow who was going to Raleigh, which was 250 miles from where I lived. He was going to a meeting downtown. He sat my trunk and me off at Hillsborough Street right beside the bell tower.

I started dragging my trunk across campus to my dorm when a man came along who helped me. It turned out that he was the senior person in my dorm and the dorm counselor. He ended up being one of my best friends. As soon as I got unpacked, I figured it was time to start looking for a job. I didn't wait until I spent the money I had, because when it ran out it would be too late. I figured the day I got there I needed to do something immediately.

All I'd heard was how hard school was, but I didn't find it that way. It was hard enough, but I didn't find it to be so terribly hard. One of the things that made it easier for me was that I feel like I got a very good high school education, even though I went to a small high school. I think there were forty-seven in my graduating class. They didn't teach all the courses that you see now. All I hear now is about magnet schools. They're teaching acting, beekeeping, and I don't know what all else at those places. You don't need but four or five things as far as I'm concerned. You need to learn to read and write and do a few other things. They didn't teach but two math courses in my school, so in four years I only had two courses.

There were five or six of us in my class who thought we wanted to go to college, and I remember I had a teacher, Ms. Marietta Smith, who was the best teacher I ever had in my life. She retired two or three years ago and the state math magazine dedicated that issue of their magazine to her. I wrote the article that they printed. This is what I said:

> *When we were younger and of school age, we thought we had the world by the tail and knew everything—that was me exactly, when I went to Mars Hill High School. The school play, athletics, goofing off and girlfriends were the highest priorities. School was OK, but not that important.*
>
> *Then came Miss Smith and math of all kinds—square, round, triangles, funny things like pi. All of a sudden it became a challenge and then fun. No matter how well we did, how much of the book we covered, there was always more, more, more.*
>
> *Miss Smith also challenged us to do better in other things. If we did not have what we needed, she helped. If we didn't have a ride, she would arrange one.*

When I went to N.C. State to study
engineering, I was in my sophomore year in
mathematics before we got to anything new to me.
Through the years Miss Smith's influence has
always been a constant in my life. When I think
about the people who have meant the most to me
through the years, Miss Smith is always among
the first to come to mind.

In study hall she would take time to teach us more advanced math beyond the two courses that were offered. We didn't get credit, but when I came to State, I placed out of the first few math courses that were required. Boys from Myers Park and all those fancy places in Charlotte had four years and didn't place out. But it wasn't because I was smart; it was because of one person who cared enough to help us.

The first job I had at State was in the dining hall. Anybody could get a job there. While you were looking for a job you could work in the dining hall. I figured early on it was OK to look for a better job, but you shouldn't quit the job you had while you were looking, especially if you liked to eat. I like to eat real good, so I worked there.

Some of my buddies knew I was looking for a job and told me about a better job at the dairy farm milking cows. I started working there, which meant I'd get up at 3:30 or 4 and go milk cows. I thought, "Well, that's good, but it would be nice to learn a little more about what I want to do in life." I didn't want to milk cows forever.

I got a job working for a professor in our department. I learned a lot about how to fasten things, wood to wood, metal to metal, and other building techniques. After that I worked over where they did all the publications for the college and did some sketching, blueprinting, and drafting. I started working the blueprint machine and drafting and that's where I learned to draw house plans and other things. I didn't learn that in class. I'm not sure I even had a professor who knew how to draw plans. But yet people will say there's no benefit to working while a kid is in college.

Every year at the state fair they had a feature exhibit. One year they were going to feature dairy. They had a big place, twenty-four feet by ten feet, as you'd enter Dorton Arena where the exhibit was. They wanted to know if I would help them build it. I made a contract to build that feature exhibit, having never built one in my life. I loved to do model work and landscaping. There was a place over on Hillsborough Street that sold balsa wood, so I could buy it at a size to fit the building scale. People used it to make model airplanes out of but I used it to make buildings. I made that display and one of the things in it was a dairy barn cut away to show the inside workings. A company that made dairy milking equipment came by and wanted to know if I'd make eighteen models, one for every district they had. They were going to give them to their salesmen to show prospective buyers. The company agreed to pay me $150 apiece. I could make one in a Saturday afternoon. I thought I was rich. Geez, I just had to make one each Saturday.

After that job, I noticed that all the guys I knew were sending their laundry out. The laundry man would come and he'd lose your stuff or get your order confused and it was a big mess. I started picking up people's laundry at the frat house where I lived, but I didn't have a car. I made a deal with the laundry and they'd come and pick up the laundry. If it cost $1, they'd do it for sixty percent of what I could collect. If a guy had a shirt or pants or two and it was worth a dollar to clean it, he'd give me a dollar and I'd have forty cents left over. So, I was doing pretty well with twenty or thirty boys living there.

I thought I could be doing better, though, so I wondered what they were doing at the other fraternity houses and dorms. I signed up a bunch of them, and I couldn't keep up with them by myself. So I got a man in each place to do the picking up, and I'd walk around and collect it. I gave the guy in each house twenty percent. I'd go to the dorms and pick up the clothes and then I'd send them to the laundry. I made twenty percent on all of those houses, so I thought I was doing really well then. Twenty percent of ten or so houses was better than forty percent of just one. I wasn't doing much more work than I had been doing for the one frat house, but I was making a bunch more money. That seemed like a good deal to me.

During this time, I was active in several campus groups, especially my fraternity. I made many friends, including Bert Brown, the best friend anyone could ever hope to have. I was a junior then, getting ready to be a senior, I hoped. A guy got sick who was an engineer who worked downtown for the state and they couldn't find anybody to replace him. He was planning on being back in a year. They just wanted to hire someone temporarily. A professor suggested I do the job, so I wound up being a full-time engineer for the department down there. Since I couldn't work regular hours because of school, I worked full-time Saturday and Sunday and nights during the week and two afternoons. I got paid like I was a regular full-time engineer.

Some of the work that I had to do was surveying. I needed someone to help me with that because someone had to carry the stick. This was about the time that I was getting serious with this girl named Jo Ellen. With all the jobs and everything, there wasn't a whole lot of time to spend dating.

I didn't get to see her as much as I wanted, because I was working most of the time. She learned in a hurry that she had to be very flexible. She would help me by carrying the survey rod on Saturday and Sunday afternoons. On

Monday, we had to go back to school. Around this time, the Air Force ROTC decided I had to learn to fly a plane before graduation. I had to practice two mornings per week, which meant I was out there around 5 or 5:30. When I wasn't flying, I'd go pick up Jo Ellen before class at Meredith College, where she was a student (and is now a trustee). We did most of our dating at breakfast. I knew right then that if I had someone that would meet me at five in the morning and carry survey rods, then I better latch on in a hurry.

When I graduated from college, I had money in the bank from all those jobs. All you hear now is about new programs for poor people who can't do anything. If it's not that, it's student loans. What "student loan" really means is a loan that won't ever be paid back. Where I'm from, we call that stealing. I have no use for that whatsoever. I hear that and I just figure, "Shucks, what are they talking about?"

I don't know that I've ever done anything I'm much prouder of than working my way through school and having money in the bank. I'm sure my kids were prouder than I was of the fact that they didn't ask me for any money to go to school themselves. They worked for it like I did. That's affected them today and the way they run their businesses.

If you didn't ever do any of those things, you wouldn't have anything to be proud of, and that's when you get in trouble. It seems like now if we have to put the pressure on anybody to go out and do something they're proud of, we feel sorry for them. The real truth is we've done them a big favor by teaching them to do something on their own. If you've ever seen anybody who really worked hard, when they get finished they've never felt that good. Nobody ever gave you anything or you've never dressed up and gone anywhere that felt as good as doing something on your own. We're replacing self-reliance, confidence, and risk-taking with "gimme gimme." This year the President made his State of the Union address and I didn't hear anything about the state of the union except that he's got lots of new programs that are going to help us all. I never heard him mention anything about us helping ourselves.

I looked around at him and others and I didn't see anybody that was a lot smarter than me that I wanted to tell me how to spend my money. I figured that out when I was buying pigs. I know how to spend my money. I don't need anyone to do it for me. I don't know what I could've done that would've helped my kids any more than instill in them a sense of doing something for themselves. They don't wait on others, they know how to do it and get on with it.

• • •

I went through ROTC when I was at State and then entered the Air Force in 1958 after I graduated from college. That was thirteen years after World War II. By the time I got out of school and was commissioned as a second lieutenant, you didn't have to go in the service if you didn't want to, but it was still considered something very special if you could get in, because people were still very patriotic. We thought we were doing something good for the country. Even after my wife and I found out I didn't have to go, I still wanted to stay in the armed forces. I worked very hard to keep up my grades to ensure that I could stay in the program. I thought it would be the greatest thing in the world to fly a plane. I thought it was something to look forward to.

Unfortunately, it didn't work out. They changed the length you had to stay active from three years to five years and I didn't want to stay that long. I was assigned to supply and material instead. I heard someone say the other day that the biggest difference in our country from then to now is that back then you lied to get in the military and now you lie to stay out of the military. That's a really big change. It was so important to all of us to do our part and now we've got people doing everything they can to try and avoid it. Even the President lied to stay out of the military. That's just a great example to be setting for our children, isn't it?

I was sent overseas and I arrived in Paris on July 14, 1958. Well, July 14th in Paris, which I didn't know at the time, was Bastille Day. I had no idea what that was. There were about 150 GIs on the plane going to airbases all over the place. Some major pulled up with a couple of sergeants and told us there weren't any trains running. They were stopped for three days because everyone was celebrating. He handed me a bunch of MPOs, which are things an officer can sign saying you can spend money. In the armed forces, they're the same as money. They gave me that and told me to take care of getting the men off the plane, find them a room, feed them, and point them in the right direction.

I thought, "I'm a second lieutenant, I can't speak French, and I've never been here before. How am I supposed to do all this?" This sergeant came up to me. He was married to a French girl, so he knew a little bit of the language and said he'd help me. That was when I learned what Bastille Day was. Half the streets were blocked and they were dancing in the streets. I didn't have any idea that it was going to be like that. It was a long way from Asheville, which had been my idea of the big city up to that point. It was the first time I had ever been out of the country.

I eventually got all those GIs straightened out and went to my assignment at the airbase in France, which was in Alsace. It was really in Germany and France, and they changed money while I was there from marks to francs because Germany had to give it back after the war. I had a lot of French civilians who worked for me. They didn't work as hard as I thought they ought to. I guess you could say we had a "culture conflict."

They took a two-hour lunch break. I tried to change that one time and that went over about like nothing. That was the first time I had ever been around what I thought was socialism. When I was growing up in Madison County, right on the Tennessee border, I'm not sure that until I got out of high school I knew anyone that wasn't a Democrat and a Baptist. I didn't know of any church near me that wasn't Baptist. We just thought people did things a certain way. It was rumored that there was a man in town who played golf. We thought he was an oddball or something. We didn't know anybody that played golf or tennis. We played baseball or basketball or football, you know, the real sports. To get to France and see all this going on was something really different to me.

I thought the French people were impossible to motivate. Maybe I didn't understand the way to motivate them. One time we went to see this fellow who owned a bakery. We'd been getting bread shipped over and one of my jobs was purchasing stuff from the local economy. This man's dad had made four hundred loaves a day, his granddad had made that many a day, and he didn't see any use in him making more than that per day. That was really different from what I was used to.

If he had made more loaves, he could have made more money and it would have accomplished two things: more money for him and more food for the hungry people I had to feed. You'd think that would interest him, but you'd be wrong. That would have been like if when I had grown that corn back home, I could have grown a whole field but I decided instead that I'd rather only grow half a field. Can you imagine anyone doing something that foolish? This man sure could.

I went over to Germany, where I was on temporary duty occasionally. I saw women running the bulldozers and things being rebuilt everywhere. It was already prettier than France and I thought, "Well, who won the war?" De Gaulle was in power at that time and a lot of people didn't like him. He was the one who finally made the Americans take the airbases out of France. As a matter of fact, my last job in France was to close the airbase where I was stationed. I thought I understood de Gaulle. He really thought the people needed something to be proud of. He never told me this, but I got the impression he thought about like I did.

You couldn't keep looking forward to working for the government or riding on the railroad with a free ticket, and not go out and work for a living. I always figured if I had one of anything, two would be better. It seemed like none of the things I thought were important mattered any to those people. They were satisfied to just do the minimum. You'd see in the paper that people were protesting things. That's what people do when they're slack and not doing anything else, because they want something for nothing. Every time I see a protest I think, "There's a big herd of people who could be off being productive if they weren't so lazy."

• • •

There was this girl who worked for me on the airbase. She was thirty or so. She was Jewish, and before the war when Hitler was being so mean to all the Jews, she saw her mother and daddy taken away. She and her family both were put in a concentration camp. One of her jobs while she was in the camp was to get people to go into a big shower and take their clothes off. She knew that they were being killed in there, but she had to do it; it was her job. It's hard for Americans to imagine having to do something like that. It could have been her family members that were going into that shower. She had lived through it, though, and she was young. I guess she was about fifteen at the time. Jo Ellen and I would talk to her about the war, and sometimes we'd go with her to some of the old concentration camps. My wife and I both got caught up in that. You could go with her and she'd tell you what she remembered.

I remember one instance that really struck home to me that the Nazi regime had been a real thing, not just something we read about in history books. The people over there liked to hunt a lot. The base commander or some other big dignitaries on our airbase would be invited to go with the mayors of the small towns on hunting trips. Our base commander didn't like to hunt that much, so he'd often give me that job. I got to go hunting a lot and it was very enjoyable.

One time we went hunting way back in the mountains on a real cold day. The Catholic priest liked to hunt and he was in our group. They put me up on this old deer stand and put him in one right down below that. It was an old wooden thing and had a top on it. It was real old looking, but I couldn't believe anyone would have a deer stand that fancy. We kept looking around and started talking. We came to realize that it was one of the guard stations that had been in the corner of one of the concentration camps.

It was unbelievable that we were just out there hunting right on the same site where there had been a camp. We'd be kicking around in the woods and find concrete ditches and other signs that that's where the camps had been. It was amazing to think of all the horror that had gone on there and now here we were enjoying ourselves and sitting up in a guard station and calling it a deer stand. That really touched me.

I'd try to figure it out, and I figured that on some days they'd have to kill 12,000 people a day. Well, nobody seemed to know it was happening. Having been in the pulpwood business when I was small, I had spent a lot of time loading one hundred pound sticks of wood one at a time, similar to what they would have had to do with the bodies of the Jews they were killing. I knew from loading the wood that just the logistics of it would be a nightmare.

If you dug a hole for the bodies, how big a hole would it have to be? How in the world could that have happened?

There was a man in Kiel, Germany, who worked on my car sometimes. He had one leg, because he lost the other one when his tank was blown up when Patton came through there during the war. His twin brother was in the tank with him and was killed. I had fished with him some and I thought he was the nicest man. I'd wonder how anyone that was so nice could have treated anyone that badly. What were they thinking about? The country's not that big, not more than a couple of states. Where could you go to do all those things that no one would see you? Somebody had to see someone doing something somewhere.

I kept trying to make some sense out of what had happened. Even where I was from, at least we'd cross the mountain once in awhile to see what was happening on the other side, even if we had to walk. It wasn't like we were totally oblivious to what was going on. How could they do all that and no one know?

You'd ask around in Germany and it seemed like everyone thought a Nazi lived next door or worked down the street, but they didn't really personally know one. Where were all the Nazis? In a secret underground tunnel or something? I never did understand it until a few years ago. Despite Clinton's actions, his approval ratings are staying around seventy or eighty percent. It's not that people don't care, but they have no trouble whatsoever overlooking or rationalizing things if they have a good job and are making money. Everything looks rosier when you're in the black.

I was reading *The Greatest Generation* by Tom Brokaw. It made a lot out of how tough people were back at the time of the war and how enduring and unselfish they were. I like to think that maybe that was my family and maybe to some extent it was partly me, even though I was young at the time.

But I look around now and I see that those same people are the ones on Medicare, Medicaid, Social Security, and those people from the "greatest generation" are the ones that have thrown in the towel. They're the same ones that when Clinton was elected, listened to all the scare on the radio and TV and were worried about something being taken away from them and voted straight ticket for the Democrats. They're the ones giving him such high approval ratings, because they're afraid if they don't vote him back in, something will be taken away from them.

I sure have a hard time seeing how that would be the greatest generation ever. They may have started well, but they're ending like a bunch of wimps. I hope there is better to come. I guess the lesson should be that they were the greatest, but look what handouts did to them. They've changed from the greatest to sitting there with their hand out.

Hitler came up around times like that. Times were bad and he gave people jobs and work. How could it be that the same thing that happened to them is happening to us now? I wouldn't say that Clinton reminds me of Hitler, but I would say that people seem like they don't care if the ends justify the means.

I was on a debate team one time and we debated whether the end justifies the means. I can't believe any nice, smart, honest, Christian person could ever be in favor of that, but it seems like our country has decided that that's the right way to be. Why would you want anyone up there just because, "I know it's bad, but I do have a good job." That's not a reason to vote for anybody. You're supposed to look at the way they act and how they treat people and what they're in favor of doing for America.

That had to be the type of attitude in Germany when Hitler came along. Those people had to see those Jews being persecuted, or at least know about it. I don't think people hated them, I don't think they liked to see people killed. They just somehow rationalized that that was a necessity to get what they wanted. That made it OK. People used to say, "That could never happen here." You can't say it would never happen when it's happening now. Think about it and tell me when's the last time you saw someone who wanted to stand up and be counted?

People will probably say, "Here we go again." But I've seen it happen in real life. Several years ago I built a house for a man from Chile. The man was the largest private employer in Chile; he had a textile plant. He had two boys that were college-aged and he sent them to Raleigh to go to NCSU to study textiles. One day he woke up and the Russians were knocking on his door. They gave him until noon to be out of his giant house he had in Chile. They also took his business. The Russians told him that his house was now their embassy and he was gone. They didn't arrest him, but they threw him out. They changed currency, so he didn't have a way to get his money. He was thrown out of his home and was broke.

He had a brother-in-law who worked for a bank in Chile who had left a message, which he didn't understand. His brother-in-law was running with the money that he was able to get out of the bank. He said he'd try and see him sometime later. They got some of their money out and things eventually worked out for him.

My wife used to tell me that if I didn't quit talking to him I'd never finish his house, because I loved talking to him. He'd be in tears and say, "For two or three years they told me to go to meetings and asked for donations because they said the Communists were coming. They were a real threat, and I said no, because I was doing so well that I thought those bad things would be impossible." He said he wished he could tell the world what happened to him. We ought to listen to people like that more, because that can happen to us.

When I grew up, I couldn't believe people were like that. We were always so strong-willed and we spoke our minds from an early age. Right or wrong, things were black or white. I know things aren't always black and white, but surely we haven't gotten to the place where there's no such thing as black and white.

It's like that joke about that little girl that wrote Clinton a letter that said, "Please help me with my mom. My mom has taken away some of my rights and makes me stay two hours a day in timeout. All that happened was Mom's vase got broken. She asked me if I broke it, and I said, 'No, I didn't break the vase.' She said she was sure I did it and I said no. I said, 'I was throwing a ball, and the ball hit the vase, and the vase fell on the floor and broke, but I didn't break it.' My mom said I threw the ball so I'm guilty and she put me in timeout. You've taught us, Mr. President, that if we choose our words carefully, we never do anything bad. Please call my mom and tell her that I didn't break the vase." I don't know whether I'm old-fashioned or a fogey or whatever, but I can't believe we've gotten to the place where we don't care if things like that keep happening.

Chapter 4
How to Live with a Red Dot Overhead

The first job I had when I got out of the Air Force helped me come towards the realization of how much I believed in free enterprise. I went to work for Carolina Power and Light Company. It was a good job and I liked working there. The people were nice to me, but I came to realize that they thought they were the bastion of free enterprise. That's all they would talk about. They even had a speaker's bureau that would go around putting on programs about free enterprise. That's all nice and fine if they could have backed it up, but when you really look at it, they had very little to do with the free enterprise system.

There were also rural electric cooperatives at the time, which the government had set up during the Depression. A lot of people in rural areas did not have electricity and, of course, many of them wanted and needed it. But, a lot of the private companies didn't see that they could be fair to their stockholders and spend the money to go into areas where they couldn't make any money. Oftentimes they'd lose money by going into rural areas.

So, as usual, the government got involved. They saw fit to set up rural electric cooperatives. They helped them go to the rural areas by giving them free loans and low-interest loans. That way, the cooperatives could afford to go in the areas that the private companies didn't want to go. They were started for a good reason. As they did better and better, they wanted more territory. But CP&L wanted some of that same territory and some of those same customers. CP&L made this big deal about how they were free enterprise and they were not the government like the cooperatives. We were supposed to go around singing that song to help them get that territory and those customers.

CP&L was a public utility. I came to the realization that they couldn't even spell free enterprise. Free enterprise is a long way from what a public utility is. Being a public utility, if you're smart enough and keep the books right, is just a way for you to collect your money. You can't lose with a public utility unless you're really, really bad at what you're doing. The utilities commission decides what your rates can be. They're political appointees and tend to follow their own prejudices, biases, and agendas.

On several occasions recently, we've had dealings with the commission or the commission's staff. When you could get past the staff and to the commission, they really tried to be fair. But I found the public staff to be something else. I'm sure that they must think they're doing a good job and looking out for the public interest, but my experience is that nothing could be further from the truth. I've found them very unorganized, lazy, inefficient, opinionated, and they play very loosely with the truth.

When I was growing up, I thought people were pretty happy. While I was at CP&L though, the government decided that areas of several states, including North Carolina, were going to be called Appalachia. They decided it was a poor place and nobody had food or other necessities, so it was time for them to get involved and set things straight.

It's funny how the government keeps records and how they always just happen to pick out a place where they can get involved. I think a lot of times there is some good reason for them to get involved, but then the wrong kind of people try to make a case where oftentimes there's not a case to be made.

Being familiar with the people from up in the mountains, I knew how well they lived. They all weren't on salary and they didn't keep explicit records of all the selling and trading they did. The government used their own methods for proving how poor the people were. The people were actually doing pretty well. That didn't fit the government's plan, though, so they had to change things around and make it look different than reality.

Most of the people who lived in the mountains chose to live there. Some of them settled there during the Civil War because they were independent minded and weren't for the North or the South. But the government was convinced that we needed the Appalachia Commission and all these other programs because the area was poverty-stricken and deserved special consideration.

I call it developing a poor-me syndrome. It's happened in a lot of places, but I'll tell you that it's also happened up there where I used to call home. They no longer have the great pioneering spirit that I thought I knew. It's really changed. When you look at the newspaper up there, half of the articles are about grants being applied for. Just think what that does to your insides over the long haul. Instead of being a go-getter and taking pride in yourself, you start looking for a grant. People never would have thought of that until the government told them it was a possibility. Then they felt like they deserved and needed it.

Through the years there have been several commissions, but the granddaddy of them all was the Appalachia Commission. At the first meeting, North Carolina's governor asked another man and me if we would go and represent North Carolina. The first meeting I went to was at 1625 Connecticut Avenue in Washington, D.C., right across from the hotel where President Reagan was shot.

You never know what to expect at these meetings. I had been out of the military only two or three years, and here I was going to Washington, D.C., where they were supposed to see all, know all, and hear all. We sat down around this table. I thought I was going to sink down to the floor when I sat in that seat, because it was so soft. There were eight states represented by a total of sixteen people.

The man in charge was Mr. Sweeney. He came in and made a talk. Then they brought in equipment fancier than any I had ever seen—audio, video, screens coming down from the ceiling, all this.

A California company was in charge. It was really an outstanding presentation. They finished and asked, "What do you think?"

I said, "Well, let's go back to number twelve or fourteen or whatever it was. That red dot up there is supposed to represent the area where poverty is the greatest, right?"

That red dot was right over my house, which I thought was a pretty interesting place to put it. "Is it really that bad there?" I asked him.

He said, "You just don't know, Mr. Ammons. You can't imagine living the way those people live."

I wanted to tell him that it wasn't too hard to imagine it, since I basically grew up right underneath that red dot. Of course, it turned out that they had never even been there. They flew over it in a helicopter or something. But they were trying to tell me, who had lived there, how bad it was.

Needless to say, we were at an impasse early on. Most of the people there seemed to agree with me. They knew what it was like where they had been and they didn't feel as though they needed the government to tell them about it. They knew that this was not a very good representation of the facts and that people from California shouldn't come up with a way to solve their man-made problems and then spend money.

It soon became evident that spending money was already past the go/no-go stage. The government was going to spend the money come hell or high water. It looked like the best thing for us to do was to come up with solutions that enabled the money to be spent for something worthwhile instead of for consultants and studies. We worked very hard to get the money spent on roads and medical facilities and a few other things we thought were lasting. It's just another example of how the government tries to solve a problem by talking people into thinking they have a problem.

I wanted to do something that I really did consider free enterprise. Plus, I never did care for working for a big company. I told some of them when I left that I wanted a job where I could work full time. They said, "You work full time here." No, I didn't. I spent a third of the day getting permission to do what I wanted to do. I spent a third of the day doing it. And then I spent a third of the day making sure they knew I did it so they'd give me a pay raise. You're only working a third of the day and that's what big companies do. That type of working does well for some people but I've never been one of them.

I remember one time CP&L sent me to a seminar. The purpose was to see if they wanted to give that seminar to everybody in middle-level management. One other man and I were sent to test it out. Basically, we were the guinea pigs. The seminar was about how to manage. I came back to the Monday morning meeting, which was with the executives of the company. The other man gave a great flowing report saying how it was the greatest thing since sliced bread and all that. Then they asked me what I thought, and I said, "Well, I don't know."

They said, "What do you mean?"

I said, "To tell you the truth, I think it would be the worst thing the company ever did. It teaches you that responsibility and authority go hand in hand. In this company, it's very clear that you want people to be responsible for everything yet you give them no authority. If they came here and taught that course, you'd have a bunch of frustrated people."

I got some real stares, I'll tell you that. They must not have listened to me too much, because they did the seminar for everyone anyway.

• • •

Right around this time is when I formed a lot of my beliefs about taxes. It really bothered me when I read about Social Security and those types of programs. What they visualized then is nothing like it is today. It was going to be one or two percent of your income. Now, it's like fourteen or fifteen percent of everything we get our hands on. It's growing now, growing this year. It's growing faster than taxes—even though in reality it is taxes—and they're growing too.

Fifty-three percent of the population doesn't pay any income taxes, and half pay more in Social Security than they do in income taxes. One percent of the people pay thirty-two percent of the taxes. That's up from twenty-nine percent the year before, even though they were making just sixteen percent of the total adjusted gross income. In other words, they were being forced to pay double the rate. The top five percent paid fifty-one percent although they only made thirty percent of the adjusted gross income, and the top twenty-five percent paid eighty percent of all the taxes in America.

Those with incomes over $75,000 bear sixty-three percent of the total income tax burden. The top twenty-five percent of taxpayers, who have incomes over $43,000, pay eighty percent of the taxes. That's important to keep in mind when we hear, "The upper-income people don't pay enough." You know who says that? People not in the upper-income bracket, and they say it because they have no clue about any bracket other than their own.

All you ever hear when they're proposing an across-the-board tax cut is that the upper-income people will benefit. Of course they will, because they're the only ones paying anything. I thought I was in a country where you got one vote no matter how much you made, and everyone got the same opportunity. I took risks with the pigs and the laundry business and bought some land and took a risk on losing it. I built a house and hoped some people would come buy it.

These people complaining didn't do any of those things. When I work hard and make money, they want my money. The only way you can get elected is to have people vote for you, and the only way it seems they'll vote for you is if you give them somebody else's money.

The have-nots or the pay-nots can outvote the haves, and I don't see anything changing. The people in power don't seem to care. They want to keep getting reelected and they don't care how they do it. Clinton made his State of the Union speech the other night. Afterwards a man called in to the radio station to comment. He said he was a computer whiz and he had machines that were smarter than most people. He had put all of Clinton's speech into his computers and figured that Clinton had given a handout to all but 317 people. He couldn't figure out why those 317 weren't as mad as they could be. He was kidding, but it was so true. Clinton gives something to every little group and individual, but he never talks about taking it away from anyone. He just keeps giving. Do the people that are getting the handouts never stop to think about where the money is coming from? If the whole setup doesn't amount to buying votes, I don't know what else to call it.

You hear we have a surplus. You'd think, "That's great, I can save more, give my kids more." No, it doesn't mean that to the government. It doesn't mean we have to pay less or that we get back what we've paid. We'd rather give our money to some of those people in Washington, whoever they are, because they're smarter than us and they can tell us how to spend our money. If we spend it like they tell us, they'll even let us have a little back.

One of the great revelations in my life came when I was growing up in the mountains. When I was in FFA, we had to memorize who the governor and other elected officials were. You'd always picture them as very smart people. I can't imagine a greater revelation than getting down to Raleigh and getting to know many of them. You find out that things aren't all right and that they're never going to be all right with those people in power. Who you thought were the smart ones scares you to death all of a sudden. There's no one looking out for me. I can't imagine anyone making a better decision for me than me. But those same people are telling me I haven't got enough sense to spend my own money. What I'd like to know is what kind of qualifications they have to spend other people's hard-earned money.

That doesn't mean I haven't had some people that have helped me along the way, though. Early on, right after I decided to go into the building business, an appraiser came out from one of the savings and loans to look at a house I was going to build. His name was Mr. Davidson and he started a construction business in Raleigh. He took some interest in what a young man starting out was doing. I remember he told me, "Well, you don't have to be very smart to get enough good jobs to make a lot of money. But you have to be really smart not to get enough bad ones to lose it."

I've repeated that hundreds and hundreds of times. I found that so true when I went in the building business. You could think you were doing so well with Job A and Job B and Job C, and then you wanted all the jobs, all the way down to Job Z. You soon learned, though, that you could get so many jobs that you couldn't make anything doing them. It sounds like it doesn't make sense, but it does. If you spread yourself so thin that you're not doing your best at anything, what's the point of trying? Sometimes you weren't sure whether you were bidding with your ego or with your brains.

I remember another man who worked in a mortgage banking company. He gave me my first three loans when I decided to go into the building business. I had no experience, I had saved $25,000, I had quit my job, and I had three little kids. I went in and told him I knew how to do it, but I had no way of proving I knew how to do it. I had some lots I wanted to build on and he trusted me enough to help me get that money to start those houses. I won't ever forget what he did to help me.

I've tried since then, not as much as I should have, to do the same type of thing. I'm glad that I've been able to help quite a few people start their own businesses—builders, contractors, plumbers, all kinds of people. I don't know how many people I've known who worked for someone else and wanted to open their own business. We were able to help some of them. Most of them still own their own businesses and now we hire them to do work for us. There's not much that will make you happier than looking around and seeing people that you helped get started in their own business. I've already seen that some of the ones we helped are now helping other people start their businesses.

Starting a business isn't all pleasure, either. Small business owners have to put up with a lot. I've got it worse than some people, because I seem to be in a lot of businesses that the government tries to control. What it's done is given our companies vast experience with dealing with the government on many levels.

The small business owner has many things to do. You have to be your own insurance agent, your own agent for dealing with the government over equal opportunity and sexual harassment, your own lawyer, your own accountant, and on and on. Most people work at a company that has specific people to deal with each of those issues. When you open your own business, you deal with all those issues yourself and you have to devote time to each one of them. Small business owners have no idea if they're breaking the law or the rules, because there's no one to ask. You don't know that you're breaking a rule until someone shows up to tell you. I think half the world is out checking to see if the other half is breaking the law. They think they've got some mandate to protect the public, so they want to tell everyone what to do.

If they had their way, all people would do would be make legislation. There are all kinds of things set up to enable legislation. The Bar Association, the Board of Realtors, the Contractors Association—there's hundreds of them. Those people get to where they have their own little dynasty. They decide how they want the world to work.

It used to be, when a CPA did your taxes, he told you he hoped it was right and if it wasn't, he'd help you. Then it got to where he had a sentence you had to sign that protected his butt if he messed up and you got screwed. Now he's got a three-page letter. You have to sign the letter because the association says it's necessary. When did the association start making rules and regulations?

They think once you make a rule that it becomes a pseudo-law. It's time to throw out some of those rules. Several years ago North Carolina decided to have a Sunset Commission. It meant that everything had run out. All those handmade rules and laws were finished. The Sunset Commission said you had to re-justify your existence since there were too many rules and laws, which sounds like a good idea.

I went to one meeting that had to do with architects and engineers. They'd decided that buildings over $10,000 had to have an architect's seal or you couldn't get a building permit. Here I was drawing my own plans, putting up my own buildings, and I couldn't do it anymore. I went to the hearings with a short-sleeve shirt on, and there were two lawyers with ties on and 180 or 190 architects with ties on telling them why they wanted the government to make laws to help them make money. They didn't think about me needing or wanting their business. They figured they wanted protection to the point that I had no choice but to hire them. That's not quite the American dream.

A committee member who raised chickens asked me during the hearing what I thought about it. I said, "If you want to get an architect for your chicken house, you go ahead and pass this." It ended up that it didn't pass. I don't know where we've come from thinking that all this is necessary. I'm sure they thought that they were protecting somebody, but on the bottom line they're just protecting their jobs. I don't know when we'll see through that.

Instead of someone that wants to buy a house from me going to see what kind of license I have, I don't know why they don't go and talk to someone that I built a house for and find out if it fell down or didn't fall down. That seems to be the right question to be asking. I could have all the licenses in the world, but you can't hold a house up with licenses. You have to know what you're doing.

The Bar Association did the same thing several years ago. They even said that lawyers couldn't advertise. Even more importantly, they set all kinds of rules. I asked one attorney to give me a reduced rate for quite a few loans that we were closing, since we were building in the same subdivision, and the title only had to be searched one time. He showed me this letter from the Bar Association outlining the percentage schedule of charges and said it would be against the rules and even unethical to reduce the rate. Boy, that's really a great example of free enterprise.

It's hard to run a small business when you have to wear so many hats. The people that are coming to check on you only have to wear half of a hat. They only have to worry about Sentence 12, Line 3, Paragraph 3. That's their whole life and yet they expect you to know as much about it as they do. You have to adopt a position that you're not scared of anybody. It's easier to ask for forgiveness than for permission, especially when you don't know who to ask for permission. Most of the things people would tell you, like government regulators, are based more on their opinion than on the law. You just have to take the bull by the horns and run over them.

I had a man over at my office recently who wanted to buy a lot from me and build his own plumbing business. He didn't know how to get a permit or get started, but he moved down here and started his own business and had thirteen employees, so he was doing well. I took an hour and talked to him about how to get started. I made a couple of calls for him and drew something for him.

It makes your day to find someone like that who has the nerve to do something for himself. It passes making your day. You could skip eating to do that. You don't see enough people that really want to get out and do something.

In situations like that, I like to share things that I've learned over the years. For example, you shouldn't price yourself out of the market. You can't get greedy. Just because things are selling well doesn't always mean your prices are too low.

It is not too hard to get momentum. If you ever price yourself out of the market or do anything else to take yourself out of the market and lose momentum, it's almost impossible to get it back. It's hard to get it when you're starting, but it's even harder to get it back. You've already got a reputation that you're not selling. So you don't want to get greedy.

But by the same token, it's important to try and make some money. Dividing up something is never a problem. Dividing up nothing is always tough.

People who are starting out in the business world don't always know these things. I like being able to help them look at all the angles and see the possibilities.

I like to help people start things because I know that I had help when I was getting started. The Lowe's Companies, especially Bruce Ballard, really helped me a lot when I started off. I was fascinated with them and thought they had the nicest employees in the world. Later on, I bought more and more from them. They came to me one time when building was slow and all of us were having tough times. They said I could have quadruple the credit I had with them and could pay it later, because they trusted me. That helped me save money and keep building when times were so bad. You hear about big companies and how badly they treat people, but I found it to be the opposite with most of them.

Northwestern Bank also helped me. It was a good-sized bank then, but by today's standards it was a little bank. This was about fifteen years ago. When I got ready to start Springmoor, a total life care community, they said they were interested in doing business with me. They seemed different to me. They still believed they were loaning money to me, not a company or something like that. I was an individual to them. That's almost unheard of now. When they came to Raleigh, I became a pretty good customer of theirs.

We went everywhere looking for money to start Springmoor. We were turned down at nine different places. Everybody thought it was a great idea, but a great idea to a bank is: Has it happened before? Can you show me where it's happened before? Have you done it two or three times? Have you done it over a number of years?

But of course, if all that were true, then you wouldn't have to borrow the money in the first place. When I went to

Northwestern Bank, they said it sounded like a good idea. They wanted to know what kind of collateral they were going to have. We wanted to make sure that the people who came in to our community had rights. We felt if we put the bank ahead of the people that might have given us $100,000 or something and things went bad, then those people would've lost their money. For banks, it's almost unheard of to not be in the first position. But I sold them on the idea that to make it work the key point was not what position they were in, but whether or not it would be successful.

The banks now put so much stock in appraisals and feasibility studies. If you get a feasibility study or appraisal, you've got to find someone to do it. I'm sure there are a lot of good people doing that job, but it seems to me that there are a lot of people doing it that failed doing other things, like the building business or real estate or something else. A bank comes along and wants to loan money to someone with a good track record who has been building for twenty years and has been somewhat successful. They check them out by letting a guy who didn't make it do the checking out.

A man I used to work with and bank with was so proud that his bank could make money with a quarter percent spread. That was a really big thing to him. In other words, if he paid someone four percent for their money, if he got five percent then he had a three quarters percent profit. Now, banks have a hard time making money on a three and a half percent spread. What's brought that about?

I was given the opportunity not too long ago to help start a new bank. I met with the regulators and decided it wasn't for me. I'd never met with people more bossy. They had more stupid little rules and asked so many insulting questions as if they didn't trust anybody. But, boy, they had a big office with these chairs with all this stuffing in them. They were charging way too much for the bank to even be a member—maybe a half or quarter percent.

Ten or twelve years ago when building was slow, I hardly remember anything being built that wasn't a bank or a government building. The government was doing it by taking people's money. If the banks did it too, it must mean they're kin to the government.

My first attorney, Mr. W.C. Lassiter, was also a great help. He's dead now, but I met him when I was at First Baptist Church. He worried so much about details I thought were unimportant. I decided I needed an attorney like that. I was bad about putting speed ahead of everything. I knew he thought that it had to be right with a clear title and signed lien waivers and all that. He wanted to follow everything to the letter.

I thought we'd get along real well, because we were exactly opposite. We made a good team. He worried about the details and I worried about the overall project. I remember telling him I was going to quit my job at CP&L and go into the building business. That very same night he drove out to my house to try and talk me out of it. He told me I had kids and they were going to be hungry, but I didn't let him talk me out of it.

He used to help me a lot when I was trying to deal with the government. He was a former city attorney, so he had experience in that field. The government will try to get you in different ways. If they can't do it with laws, then they'll do it with rules and interpretations of rules. Most rules are made up to fit someone's opinion. I have a reputation that if you can't show it to me in black and white, then I don't agree to it and I fight it. He used to say that the government only had one way of doing business and that was through "mainstrength and awkwardness."

I disagreed. I said their main way was blackmail. I still think that's right. If the government can't get you to do something the way they want, then they'll spend all their time saying that if you don't do it, they'll make it hard to get permits, approvals, and things like that. They'll even "lose" your application and "forget" that you exist.

I remember one time in particular when I got to loving that man so much. I had a deal with a bank here in town. We were getting ready to do a project together by going in half and half. That was before I learned not to do it that way. Going in half and half with anyone more powerful than you means that their half is giving orders and making money and your half is doing work.

I was going to run it and they were going to furnish the money. At the time, I considered it to be a great big project, probably about two hundred houses. We had agreed on what we were going to do. This was early in my career and I was eager for everything to go perfectly. We got ready to make a deal and the bank jerked the rug out from under me. I had already found the land, made a deal, spent my own money, got some engineers, signed an option, all that. The bank said they weren't going to do it and it cost me my own money.

I sat around and moped for a day or two and then my wife told me to quit feeling sorry for myself and get out there and do something. So I went downtown to see the bank president. His secretary was sitting out front and she said, "You can't go in there." I've never been one to let a secretary stop me, so I went in his office anyway. I told him I wanted to talk to him about what went on. He said we'd have a meeting and he'd listen to me.

We set the meeting for a few days later. The bank's lawyer came and Mr. Lassiter came with me. The bank president also brought the man that was going to be the next president of the bank. It was the first time I had met him. Their lawyer stood up and said, "Mr. Ammons, we all know what we're here for. You don't have a leg to stand on. You don't have anything you can produce in writing to show that we didn't do exactly what we said. We're not liable for anything. These are important people and we don't need to waste their time."

After they told me that, I told them I knew that already and appreciated them taking the time to meet with me. To start with, I knew I couldn't make them do anything so I said, "I wanted to get all of y'all together in one room and tell you what a sorry bunch of individuals you are and how dishonest I think you are."

Mr. Lassiter jumped up and said, "Sit down," and he pushed me down. "I apologize for my client," he said. "There will be no more outbursts like that. But I'd like to make one thing crystal clear: I agree with him one hundred percent."

I knew right then I had found my buddy. I knew I had picked the right person to be my lawyer. Eventually, the new president of the bank felt bad about the whole situation and came to talk to me about it later. He was moving into the area from another town and I wound up building him a big house. I still see him and we made a lasting friendship in spite of the trouble we had when we started. I think when honest people disagree, it makes them closer, it doesn't tear them apart.

After we got the deal straight with the bank, I was able to do the project, even though we had to do it a different way than we had intended. Part of my deal in buying some of the land was that the man selling the land wanted to trade it for something that was income producing. He had him some Realtors, and the Realtors went around and found some property he wanted. I had to buy that property and trade it to him, in a simultaneous transaction. That way I'd end up with what I wanted and he'd have what he wanted. Now they call that a tax-free exchange.

I had a check in my pocket for a lot of money and I went down to the office where our meeting was scheduled. They had this great big old table. There were four or five different Realtors there who were representing the different pieces of land the seller wanted me to buy to do the trade. One or two of them had lawyers. Mr. Lassiter was out of town at the time and couldn't go with me.

I sat down kind of behind them. They were all around the table drinking coffee. I sat there a minute and finally asked when we were going to start. This lawyer said that they were waiting on Mr. Ammons. I said, "That's me, and I'm ready to start anytime you folks are." They made me a place at the table and then we sat there for a few more minutes. I asked, "Are we ready to start?" I still remember this conversation.

The lawyer said, "We're waiting on your counsel."

"Who?"

He said, "Your counsel."

"I don't believe I've got anybody like that."

"Your attorney. You have an attorney, don't you?" he asked me.

"Well, no, do you think I need one?"

He said, "Well, it seems to me like you do. Have you talked to anybody about this?"

"I talked to my wife about it a few minutes this morning before I left the house."

Finally he was giving in a little bit. "Well, if you're ready," he said. "But who's going to check these papers?"

"As nice and smart a guy as you are, I'm sure there will be nothing wrong with them and everything will be in order. You don't know any reason why I shouldn't trust the papers you've got, do you? I'm sure you did them just right." I kept on going, "I'm from the mountains, from Madison County. Do you know where that is?"

He looked at me kind of funny and said, "Yes, that's way up there in the mountains."

"Yeah, they call it bloody Madison. We trust everybody up there not to screw us up. If they do, we shoot them."

He said right quick, "Oh, well, I'm sure you'll find everything in order, Mr. Ammons."

I thought we had everything straightened out. "That'll be great, let me look at it," I said. I looked at it and on the first line they had my name spelled wrong and my wife's name spelled wrong. I pushed the papers back across the table and said, "Why don't we meet tomorrow and you can clean this stuff up and we'll start again then?"

Mr. Lassiter wasn't the only character I met when I was first starting out. One of the best friends I ever made was named Mr. Denson, who was seventy-eight years old when he died recently. I met him over thirty years ago. He was in the grading business and was working for someone else at the time. I needed someone to run bulldozers and grade streets and lots of things. I really did like him when I met him. He lived way out in the country and he enjoyed acting like he was a country man. He was this big ol' man who wore overalls and probably weighed three hundred pounds.

When he first started, his wife would help him run one piece of equipment while he ran another one. Eventually he had a son who helped him and a daughter too. When his son was eleven or twelve, Mr. Denson told me they'd asked his son to go to the Caterpillar manufacturing and sales plant because they wanted to make a movie of him running this giant pan that hauls dirt. You ride up on the front, way up high, and it has big wheels. It's called a push-and-pull, because it has two motors—one in the front and one in the back. The company was impressed that this young kid was able to run this piece of heavy machinery.

When they got back, I asked Mr. Denson if he had a good time. "Well, yeah, I did," he said. "They made a real big deal out of my son. I told them we should've come up there a couple years ago when he started driving it." Someone else heard about it, too, because they asked his son to come be on "What's My Line?" He stumped them all, because they couldn't guess that a little boy could drive that equipment.

One time Mr. Denson was going to build me a lake for one of my projects. It was about thirty or forty acres, which was pretty good size. We had to go to the state and talk to these people who called themselves engineers—I can say that because I'm an engineer. They had to have a pre-construction conference. We went in there with Mr. Denson's brother-in-law. They both had on overalls and looked about as country as can be. I'm sure the engineers thought we had absolutely no clue what we were doing. Those boys said that if we were going to build a lake, they wanted to know if my subcontractors, meaning Mr. Denson, had built a lake before. They said they had, so the government boys wanted to know how many they had built.

"Well, I don't rightly know," the brother-in-law said. "How many do you think we've built?"

Mr. Denson said, "I don't know. I reckon it's been four hundred or five hundred of them."

Well, that stumped them. They said, "Yeah, but y'all have been building these little teeny ones and now you have to build a big one. Have you ever built one this size?"

"Yeah we have," the brother-in-law said. "How big was that one we built down there in Bunn?"

Mr. Denson said, "I'm not really sure. I think it was about nine hundred acres."

Well, the engineers still figured they had to win. They said, "But this is going to be twenty-eight or thirty feet high. The dam is going to be an earthen dam and all that. Have you ever done that before?"

"Yeah, I believe we have," his brother-in-law said. "How high was that one we built?"

"I don't remember exactly," Mr. Denson said. "But I had to stand that pipe up there to drain it with, and I think it took three joints of twenty-foot pipe. It must've been about sixty feet high."

They eventually ran out of questions and figured out we knew a little bit about what we were doing, so they finally let us leave.

Another time there was an inspector who was giving us a hard time. Mr. Denson was the nicest man you've ever seen, but he didn't believe in wasting his time or mine. I was coming back from the farm and got a call on the car telephone. This lawyer said Mr. Denson was in real trouble. They told me the inspector was out at the site and told him he had to move the erosion device. Mr. Denson told him that it was exactly where it ought to be, that it had to be in the lowest place. It was clear that it was where it should be in order to perform its function. But the inspector thought that the map was more important than doing the job. He showed Mr. Denson the plans, which showed that it was twenty feet away from where the plans called for it to be. Mr. Denson told him, "You don't pay me, Mr. Ammons pays me, so you need to go talk to him."

The inspector told Mr. Denson he was going to stop the job and Mr. Denson told that inspector since he wasn't driving the bulldozer, he couldn't stop it. The inspector told him he was going to stand right there in front of him—they

were in front of this bank of dirt that fell off about eight feet high—and they weren't going to be able to move the machine. So Mr. Denson cranked up the machine and got about six inches of dirt with the blade of his tractor and rolled the inspector off the bank with the dirt.

That was just his way. There was very little nonsense. So when the lawyers told me, I couldn't do anything except laugh.

Another time, he called me at two in the morning. He said, "I've got a problem. I need you to come over here and pick up some stuff for me." I told him I would, but I asked him where it was. He told me to go to such-and-such a road and go to the stop sign and make a few turns. He wanted me to come right at daylight and pick up a pistol and a shotgun and take them to him.

The next day he met me for lunch and told me what happened. He had a job where people kept stealing his gas after work hours at night. They were stealing it out of his bulldozers and trucks. He decided he was going to catch them doing it. He lined up his equipment in a row the way you do when you're going to refuel it. He took a bite to eat in a bag so he could have dinner while he waited for the thieves.

Around about 10:30 a car with big tires and the back end jacked up drove up. It was making the biggest noise you've ever heard. "Whoom, whoom, whoom, whoom!" These two boys slid up to the equipment and started siphoning gas. Mr. Denson stepped from behind that machine with a five-cell flashlight and shined it right between their eyes. As he did, he pulled out a pistol and shot straight up in the air. They took off and Mr. Denson said they climbed up the bank like a bunch of squirrels.

Mr. Denson told me, "I went back over to my truck, and I looked and there was a shotgun and some shells. I said to myself, 'Layton, you need to go back over there and make sure you finished that job.' So I put them in my pocket and went down there and started shooting that car. Those big tires went 'Psssssssss' after I shot them. I figured they wouldn't come back anymore. Then I went back to the truck and there were three more shells. I said to myself,

'Layton, there's no use wasting these. I might as well finish
the job.' I stuck them back in my pocket and went back and
shot the dash out of that car."

I remember interrupting him and saying, "Wasn't the
car locked?"

His response was, "No, I had already shot all the glass
out, so it wasn't hard to get to it."

There was more to the story. He said, "One of their
daddy's called me and wanted to know if I was going to
pay for the car. Can you believe they would do that? The
deputy sheriffs came out to see me and I told them I would
never do anything like that. I asked them if people hadn't
been stealing gas out of equipment all over the county, and
they said they had had some trouble with that. I told them
I didn't know much about it, but if they would tell the other
contractors to handle it the same way someone did at this
job, it would make their job a lot easier."

The man devoted his whole life to running that
equipment. He'd done it everywhere you can think of. He
never made a contract with anybody and you knew he

would charge you less than anyone else would. I asked him one time if he ever had anyone that wouldn't pay him. It wasn't uncommon to get a bill running $10,000 or $20,000 a day. I felt sure that at some point someone had tried to get out of paying him. In a month's time with those types of bills, you can eventually start talking about big money.

He said that one time he had had some trouble with a big shot in town. "I don't work on Sundays," he said. "But I do sometimes go over and look at jobs on that day. I went up to his house before time to go to church on Sunday and tooted the horn. I told him we were going to ride over to the job he had going so that I'd be straight Monday morning. We rode over there. I knew he kept his checkbook in the office trailer. So I just pulled out a pistol and laid it up there and told him he was going to write me a check or I was going to shoot him. He went right in and wrote me a check. That's the only time I ever had trouble."

Nothing was ever a problem too big for him. He just knew his stuff. I can't ever imagine being around anyone that was a closer friend of mine than he was. There will never be another one like him.

Chapter 5
The Importance of
the Atlanta Airport

It's funny to realize how much of what I do today actually began a very long time ago. People think you just wake up one day and decide to go into the building business, but it's not like that. It's a series of progressions, and when I look back on my life, I can see how I got to where I am now.

When I was growing up, there were two or three boys who lived up the road a ways. We spent a lot of time working and we also spent a lot of time playing outside. One of the things we loved to do was make tree houses. We'd find barns or sheds or anything we could tear down to get tin or something off the top, and we'd make very elaborate tree houses. We had different kinds of steps and rope ladders and all the extras. That's probably when I got my first interest in the building business. People would always want to see the tree houses that we'd build.

My dad and some other people in town had a little sawmill. It was the kind that was movable, because you could only haul the trees and logs so far. It was pulled by a big belt and a pulley. We did a lot of logging with that mill using horses to pull them. We'd get the logs down and then saw them with the sawmill. I had a lot of interest in the wood and the sawing. It even got to the point where I liked the smell of it.

I had an uncle who used to go around and build barns for people. Back then, most of the frames for barns were built out of poles. You'd go in the woods looking for long, straight trees twenty or thirty feet long. They might be six or eight inches at the bottom, but ideally they'd be as skinny as possible. We'd use those to build the barns. These days, you buy treated lumber if you're going to put it on the ground. We just used locust trees.

Then, when I was in college, one of the jobs that I used to work my way through school was drawing plans. North Carolina State had a place where anyone that wanted to could come in and get help drawing plans or working on sketches. The first job I had was running the blueprint machine where people made copies of their plans. That was back when they were all ammonia machines, which meant you had to open a window no matter how cold it was. That ammonia will get you after awhile.

I really enjoyed doing that. As I mentioned earlier, I also had a job as an engineer while I was still in college. I knew that I had a lot of interest in blueprinting and drawing plans. While I was still working at CP&L, I built my house in Dunn. A friend of mine and I built the entire house ourselves. He helped me build mine and I helped him build his.

One thing led to another and eventually I met a guy who was working on a couple of houses. He didn't really know a lot about plans, so I started helping him get a few permits. We had a halfway unannounced partnership. We found a lady one time, who later came to live in Springmoor, who had some property in Raleigh and wanted to build some rental houses and a couple of stores. I drew the plans and went in as partners with this man. We built those houses and a little shopping center. I was starting to get in the building business without really being in the building business.

Every day I would think about it more and more. I was drawing some house plans for builders in Raleigh and it looked like I was getting more involved all the time. With the job I had at CP&L, I had to travel some and I remember one Friday I was in Atlanta. That was in the days when Eastern Airlines was still around and Atlanta was a very busy hub. They used to say that if you wanted to go to hell, you had to go through Atlanta. I was supposed to be coming home because one of my kids had a ballgame or something that I wanted to go to, but my flights got all fouled up. I wound up not getting home until the next day.

That really got to me. I said to myself, "Why am I doing this when I really want to be building?" That's when I decided to stop. You can't halfway stop; you have to fully stop. A lot of people told me it would be really dumb to stop when I had three little kids and really didn't have a business already started. They thought I was being crazy to jump into something new. All I knew was that I knew how to build and wanted to build. But you have to start somewhere, so I came back from Atlanta and told my boss at CP&L that I had enjoyed it, but that I was leaving and "Bye."

That meant I was in the building business. I went to the bank to get started. It was harder to borrow money then than it is now. I wanted money to build three houses and I got it. I'd also remodel anyone's house that wanted it remodeled. I even built a barn or two. If they'd pay me to do it, I'd do it.

We started doing three spec houses over on Ridge Road. It was the biggest thing in the world to me. I've often said that the best house I ever built was the first one. You take interest in every little thing. It's like your baby. You see everything that happens and you want it to be perfect. We wanted to save as much money and be as efficient as we could. I had this old truck that I drove around in. I'd drive around in the morning and line up everyone that was going to work and go supervise the jobs and order materials.

Around three o'clock, when things slowed down, I'd get a broom and shovel and go clean the houses myself. My wife did the decorating because she always enjoyed that. She made deals with carpet and wallpaper places to give people choices on what to put in their houses.

On the weekends, someone had to baby-sit and someone had to sell the houses. We'd take turns sitting in the houses and trying to sell them while the other one looked after the kids. By Sunday night, the whole week started over again when you started looking for people to work on Monday.

When we sold our first house, we thought God had sent the people that bought it. It had been pretty slow and it took almost a month. I know we worried those people sick. We took them flowers, took them out to dinner, and pulled out all the stops. Interest was adding up on those houses, so it was a very big deal to us. Banks charge interest on weekends, holidays, and any other day you can imagine. It never stops, even though they might not be open.

The building business is such a personal business. I've been fortunate because my whole family has been involved in it. Before Jeff went to school he would ride with me half a day out on the job. When he was five or six and started school, I thought I was going to have to keep him out of school because it was so lonesome without him. He'd ridden around with me every day and he knew the subcontractors on the job. He's building now and I bet he still remembers those days.

Our whole family played a role in the business. Instead of watching TV at night, our family used to talk about our houses. It got to the point that you almost hated to sell them because you'd put so much into it. You wanted to sell them, but you hated to see them go. That meant that the people that bought them were your friends because you felt so close to them. Everything was very personal and that made it fun. What made it more fun was succeeding, because you were doing everything yourself.

Jo Ellen had such a positive influence on me. She had a positive attitude and stayed happy all the time. She even kept the books for quite awhile. She also decorated the houses and visited the customers after they moved in to take them a plant, see how they liked it, and make sure everything was going smoothly. It seemed to surprise people sometimes when she showed up to check on them. For us, it just seemed like the natural thing to do. We worked very closely with our customers.

The people who worked for us almost became like family and we still use quite a few of them today. It was as important to make them feel good as it was to make the customer happy. It wasn't like they were just working for me—they were working for whoever wound up buying the house. If they stayed happy and we sold more houses, that meant there would be more work for them. When things go the way they should, it should be a smooth circle. We wanted everyone to feel like a family. If one succeeded, we all succeeded. Even our suppliers got to the point where they were almost like part of our family. That's how I got to be such good friends with the Lowe's Company and Northwestern Bank, who ended up being two of my very special friends.

We used to have a big lunch and barbecue every Christmas and I thought that was really fun. Everyone affiliated with our business would be there, from the job foreman down to the guy that only hammered in one nail. They'd bring their families and we'd just have a great time. Lots of people have family picnics, but we had a big family picnic.

• • •

We mentioned earlier that being a small business owner means you have to be a jack-of-all-trades. That has some disadvantages, but it also has advantages. It certainly gives you an opportunity to be more well-rounded and learn more. There are a lot of regulations to deal with though. It seems kind of silly that you have to go around and ask people if you're allowed to be in the business you want to enter. Sometimes, you just have to take the attitude that, "The hell with it, I'm going to go ahead and start. If anyone gets mad, I guess they'll show up and tell me about it."

When Jeff was at State he was taking an environmental engineering course. There were one hundred people in the class and someone from the EPA came in to talk. They said that they needed so much tax money and the need was so great for people to help them that they wished they could hire everyone in the room. Everyone started applauding, but Jeff said he kept quiet. He thought, "Yeah, they'll hire them and then they'll all be out bothering my dad tomorrow."

After we got started, I decided it was time to find someone to sell my houses instead of having to sit over there every Saturday and Sunday afternoon with the kids. So, I decided to go into the real estate business. I wanted to find someone that would be willing to take a personal interest in it.

One day, I had a house for sale and there were people looking at it. (This is back when houses were slow to sell and interest rates were high. When you got a customer, you took a keen interest in them.) It was Friday afternoon about two or three o'clock and the people had to go back to Ohio that same day. They wanted to apply for their loan before they left so they wouldn't have to come back. Needless to say, I wanted to help them as much as I could with the loan. I called the bank where we had our construction loan. They said, "It's late Friday afternoon and we're all backed up and can't do it." I needed to sell the house. The interest was running. I needed to pay off the loans I already had and I needed to build more. But they said there was nothing they could do.

I called another bank. By this time I was getting madder and madder and probably louder and louder. There was a trainee named George Pittman at one of the banks that said they didn't have time to help me. In about thirty minutes he called and said he had heard me call and knew I was upset. He said even though he was new, if I'd come to the back door at five o'clock he'd unlock the door and take my application. I knew that there were not many people with that attitude.

I went down and he took the application. I called him the following week and said, "Anyone that would take that much responsibility and do what you did for me needs to be in his own business. You don't need to be working for someone else." So, he gave notice of his resignation and we started a real estate company together. We've been partners ever since.

It was also about this time that two of the really good things that ever happened to me occurred. One was when Jo Ellen hired Sylvia Doles to come work for us. Her job was to keep the books, answer the phones, and be my assistant. Of course, sometimes she was my boss. She worked in the same office with me and listened to my loud talking and meetings with people. I don't think she's ever made an accounting error in twenty-seven years. She stays happy and positive and keeps me on the go. She and Jo Ellen became great friends and they've even been known to gang up on me.

The second good thing was when this young fellow named Mason Williams called one day looking for a job. He had no experience, wasn't married at the time, and had spent the past several years overseas and sailing a sailboat.

If you've read this far in the book, you know that some person that had been off on a sailboat for a bunch of years didn't exactly start off at the top of my list. He didn't say anything that endeared him to me too much or made me think he wanted to work too hard. But he was back in Raleigh for a while and I knew his mother and father, who also lived in Raleigh. His father was sort of the dean of real estate companies at that time.

Mason came to talk to me one day. He had long hair with a ponytail and was wearing cutoff jeans. I remember thinking, "This guy is going to be a laughingstock. I can't send him out to my job site." But he started working on one of our trash trucks, which was the dirty work. After three or four months, he started asking questions and I could tell he was really interested. One time he told me, "If I could take the plans home with me, I'd be able to study them and might be able to do a better job." That made me realize he was really doing something.

Within six months, he started being the boss. Not long after that, he was the foreman. We really became close. One time a guy was in my office and I guess he didn't want to complain about me, so he decided he'd complain about Mason. I said, "Stop it. You can say what you want to around here, but Mason is my other son, and that's off limits." I still think of him that way. We've built many things together and he's now in his own business. We accomplished a lot working together.

While he was working for us, we slowly began building bigger things, such as subdivisions. One of the things you have to do when you do those types of projects is name streets and lakes and other areas like that. It's not always an easy job. When I travel I always make a point to swipe phone books, because you have to find a name that's never been used in this county, and they run out quick. One time when I came home from work I told everyone to take an hour and go brainstorm. I wanted a name for a subdivision and a name for the streets in the development. David was eight or ten at the time and he came up with Lake Park for the subdivision. He also had names for all the streets. It was right near where the city was building Shelley Lake, so it worked out very well.

Along about this time, the late 1970s, I was very active in the Homebuilders' Association. One of the big topics, just like it always has been, was affordable housing. I was on a committee that dealt with it, and I got tired of people just talking and not doing anything. They seemed to think that if they talked about it long enough in a committee meeting that houses would magically sprout out of the ground.

So I went out on Poole Road where houses and land were cheaper and bought some land and started building more affordable houses. At this time, the average house was in the $125,000 range. These were between $70,000 and $80,000. Instead of just building one or two, we built several hundred, because we wanted to make the statement that we could do it. It was a very personal project and we didn't want it to look like a stepchild. I put in a nice entranceway and lots of amenities that you'd see in a higher-priced neighborhood. We had real good luck selling out there and what had been considered the wrong side of town turned out to not be that way at all. These days, we feel like we have a lot to do with that side of town being considered more acceptable.

Soon after that, a large tract of around five hundred or six hundred acres in that area became available. I wanted to make it into a big mixed-use park: houses, business, office, industrial, everything. I worked with the city of Raleigh and we made some deals that were designed to make it look very pretty. The city and the county were both very interested in it, because they like to increase their tax base, and at that time they didn't have a lot of places where people could put businesses. We're still not through with it, but it's gone very well. It would've been even better if it weren't for the government.

Our biggest competitor has always been the government. I'd buy land at $10,000 or $15,000 per acre, and do all the roads and sewer myself. Someone would be looking to buy a place, but they could find it cheaper at another place where the government would give them money to do water and sewer. I don't want to get going on that too much right now, because we'll talk about it later. At this point I was in my own business—buying, selling, and building on a regular basis. I was taking risks and being my own boss, even though the government liked to think they were the boss. I loved it.

Chapter 6
The First Sentence
Says It All

I used to say that the title for my book was going to be, "The first sentence says it all." How many times have you been in a meeting or classroom, or more importantly, you've interviewed someone for a job, and you can preach and preach on something and the first sentence that they say blows your mind? One time I talked to our Congressman about the Army Corps of Engineers and EPA and some rules they had about the wetlands. He invited me to come over, was nice enough to listen, and was very nice to me. I guess we talked for close to two hours and I did most of the talking.

I explained to him how dumb the rules are and how unfair they are and how most of them aren't even laws, but someone's rules, and they just enforce them as laws. I went

through that whole long spiel and I thought I was really getting somewhere and that he was really listening. I thought, "The man is getting it. Maybe he'll get as upset and as mad about it as I am." I was feeling pretty good about myself.

His first sentence when I got through—and all the time I had been talking about private property rights and people running over my property and thinking they own it and making rules about it—was "Well, I knew when Reagan and Bush came in and we got rid of a lot of career government employees that we were headed for a bad time because we didn't have the same good employees up there that we used to have."

Here's a smart man, but all he heard was that the programs weren't working like they should be. But what I'd been trying to tell him was that we didn't need the programs. It was a perfect example of how you hear from your past experiences and what you want to hear, not with your ears. If he had been paying attention, he would've known that what he was saying sounded ridiculous in the context of what I had just said. This was a United States Congressman and he didn't have a clue how to listen.

It's not just Congressmen who have a problem with listening. I remember one fella was just getting out of college with his MBA. My wife had talked to him earlier and he came to talk to me about a job. I liked him a lot, too. I was telling him about what we do and how much we like it. I told him how we like to see the grass grow and streets built and how we enjoyed the opportunity to make things look good and leave your mark.

I finished talking and he said he wanted to ask me two or three questions. I thought it was great that he would take the initiative. I was sure he had some good questions. But then he piped up with, "What kind of retirement and medical plan do you have?" Right then I figured I better just answer one or two things and get him out of there. I wouldn't have hired him then no matter what else he said. I thought we were talking about opportunity. If you don't want to talk about opportunity when you're looking for a job, why are you looking for a job? He didn't seem to care.

I think what people say, the first comment or question they have, will tell you more about the person than anything else they will ever tell you.

• • •

I can remember way back when seeing a Japanese or German car was an oddity. You might see a British car, but not very many other foreign models. UNC, State, all the government-subsidized schools were very cheap to attend because they were paid for by some hard-working person's money. The students would graduate and then I don't know what happened to them. The girls were worse than the boys. They'd gotten an education at someone else's expense. They felt like a hero for that and then all of a sudden they wanted a job. Some even demanded it because they'd "arrived." As soon as they got their job, the first thing they would do is go buy a Japanese or German car.

I'd say, "Why did you buy that? Did those people pay for your education?"

They'd say, "What are you talking about? That doesn't have anything to do with it."

Oh, really? I always figured that when the first German or Japanese person bought my house, I'd buy their cars. There's a story about a guy who worked for me who came in one day and said he'd heard that if anyone who worked for me bought a foreign car, they'd get fired. I explained to him that nothing was further from the truth. I'd never do that and anyone who told him that was wrong. However, I did fire people for poor judgment and I would consider buying a foreign car extremely poor judgment.

Seems to me that you were biting off the hand that fed you by graduating from a taxpayer-supported college and then giving your money to a Japanese or German company. You let Americans educate you, raise you, and everything else, and then you insult them by buying a major item from another country. At the shopping center we have, I go out of my way to buy from the tenants who rent from me. I'd almost kill to make sure I do business with them. If loyalty isn't important, I don't know what else you have in this world.

It doesn't take people very long to realize that loyalty is a quality I value. One time I had another partner in the real estate company. Over one weekend I had had someone make an offer on a house, and then on Monday my partner came over and had an offer on the same house. I had told the person who called over the weekend that I was doing something else, but if they bought it Monday I'd sell them the house for $2,000 less than what I was asking. I told him they had made an offer and I accepted.

My partner came in Monday morning and had an offer for full price. He told me that since I hadn't signed anything, I wasn't obligated to take the other offer. I told him there was no way I'd back out of the offer. He said my trouble was that I put loyalty ahead of making money. I told him his trouble was that he had been there two years and hadn't figured that out yet.

The following Friday at ten o'clock we met. We were going to make a give-or-take offer. My daddy had taught me a long time ago that if you were in business with anybody on anything and they wouldn't make you a give-or-take offer (in other words, I'll give you so much for your part or I'll take the same thing for my part) then they weren't worth dealing with. As it worked out, I bought his share of the business and we weren't in business together any longer.

Sometimes people really do say something good when you meet them, though. I had a boy in recently who's getting ready to graduate from college. He wants to learn the development business and someone told him to talk to me because it was a religion for me, it wasn't just being a developer. He was caught up in it. You could tell by the twinkle in his eye. He was getting in the discussions just like he was already an employee. He didn't ask about how much we were going to pay him or how many hours he'd work. All he talked about was how he thought he could help us, his vision for the future, and how he wanted to be a risk-taker.

If people just knew how much the world was crying out for that. Can you imagine a McDonald's or Hardee's where an employee would be there an hour or thirty minutes earlier than they were supposed to be or did something before you told them to? I don't believe it would be a week before they would be the boss. The world is crying for people to take initiative, to step up and do something. People come up with all these reasons why they can't. If they'd spend less time making up reasons and more time doing something, maybe they could do things right.

I remember one time I was so proud of my son, David, when he worked at Springmoor. They had a kitchen and about six hundred people ate there every day. A lady in town knew there was a lot of food being thrown away by restaurants and other kitchens. She had a dream that that food could be used to feed hungry people. She called David and asked him for some food. She already had some fast food restaurants helping her. After only a week, she was making progress. She bought an old truck, just trying to get started. After a day or two, all the restaurants stopped donating food, especially the chains which had legal departments. They told her they were taking responsibility for too much, that if someone got poisoned or sick there would be trouble. They thought it would be better to throw the food out than to let some hungry person eat it.

I'm sure they felt good about themselves because they kept their company out of trouble. They probably didn't have any trouble sleeping. She called David and told him what was happening. He told her he wasn't scared of that. So I figured at least I did one good thing in my life when I raised him. Later, the Good Samaritan law was passed which relieved the liability of people who tried to do good things. If somebody hadn't stepped up to the plate to start with, that wouldn't have happened. Now that lady feeds hundreds and hundreds of people every day in Wake County. Because of the way the legal system is, people are often afraid to help other people.

I read a book called *Megatrends* written by John Nesbitt. I was on a panel with him one time and I thought he was a pretty interesting person. He had one thing in his book that was so true. He said a lawyer was just like a beaver, because they get in the mainstream and dam it up.

I remember one time they asked Mr. Willie York, a big Raleigh developer who built the first shopping mall anyone in these parts had ever seen, to what he attributed his success. He said he never brought his attorney in on a deal until he had already made the deal. That is such a smart comment. Now people have to get an accountant and an attorney and work out a plan. What you ought to have is a burning desire and a vision to do something. The world isn't going to come down on you; just start something.

I talked to the business school at Chapel Hill once. The class was discussing how to be a developer. I guess they were looking for me to tell them steps one, two, three, and four so they could take notes and write them down. One guy in the class asked me, "Mr. Ammons, if you want to be in the development business, how would you start? Would you hire your accountant first or your lawyer or make a business plan or get an engineering degree or what?"

I said, "Shoot, I'd get a bulldozer and push something." And that's exactly what I meant. How else are you going to start? You don't start by talking about starting.

One time I was at the bank and for their training program for new employees, they wanted me to tell them what a customer expects from a bank. I made what I thought were some very good recommendations. I'm not sure they took them the way I meant them. They asked me how I would recommend they help me more. I said the first thing they could do was fire two out of three of the MBAs they send out to see me. They could double the pay of the one they kept, train him better, and give him a telephone and enough authority to tell me something when he came to see me. All they do now is get MBAs who don't know anything and don't have the authority to do anything and expect me to train them. I'm not sure they'll invite me back after that, but it was good advice.

People come to talk with you, you ask them something and they have to "get back to you." Wouldn't it be nice if someone came in the door that didn't have to "get back to you" all the time? I'd give about anything to have a meeting with someone who had the authority to actually do something.

At that same meeting one of the guys high up in the bank asked me if I'd tell them why I stay in the business when I probably don't have to anymore. He said I wouldn't have to get up early to do more projects, wouldn't have to sign any more promissory notes. He wanted to know why I kept taking the risks. I thought about it and said, "I'm not going to answer that question, because anyone that would ask that wouldn't understand the answer." I think that's right. The answer is, "That's what we do." There isn't any other answer. If that's what you do, that's what you do. He acted like it was really terrible to have to get up and do work. If you look at it that way, I guess it is. But I'd rather think of it as having an opportunity. I try not to turn down opportunity and that's why I'm still in the business.

In my office, I've got a big sign, and I guess it's our motto. It says, "Don't wish you had, be glad you did." I think that's our philosophy, that's what we're about.

• • •

We've been in a running battle for a year now with the utilities commission public staff over the sewer plant we had. Nothing we had was good enough for them. First they wanted to see our records. Then they'd tell us they were coming back and then they didn't come back. Then we'd ask them if they were through and they'd say they weren't.

Then they'd schedule a public hearing telling us that our customers needed to come. We'd send a notice to our customers to see if they had any complaints. If they complained the commission wanted to hear the complaints. Out of four hundred or so people, one wrote back and he was just questioning something. So we figured maybe we wouldn't have to have a hearing.

But the commission started talking to our customers and then thirty-two letters came in saying they didn't like what we were going to do. If you read the letter you could tell they were form letters. The public staff had passed them out and had told people to fill them out and send them in. The commission passed out those form letters and promised our customers refunds if they complained. You can't be any sorrier than that.

That's just the government trying to run over somebody. They're mean and vindictive. They don't want to solve problems. They make up their mind about what they want to happen. *If the public really knew what they did in the name of protecting them and what it was costing them, they would never want any more protection.*

If you want to get a road approved, there are a lot of things you have to do. You have to get the soil checked and plans approved and all that. Once you get all those things done, you get a letter saying the road is approved. Then you have to warrant it for one year. After that the road belongs to the city or county or state. We tried for two months to get an inspection for this one road we were working on, but they were too busy. Finally an inspector came out around Thanksgiving and did his inspection. After four or five phone calls to find out if it passed inspection, we found out it had been in the computer for a month and they just hadn't had time to type it. It was approved a long time ago. It took that long for one letter, a standard letter with two paragraphs—one with one sentence and one with two sentences. I'm sure they spent more time answering my phone calls than writing the letter. That's how our days go. Fight, fight, fight.

One of the first lessons I learned was about zoning. In Raleigh, everything has to be zoned. Land is zoned for certain purposes. If I have land, it could be zoned for apartments, let's say. Somebody will then decide that it's some sort of critical area, which can mean a lot of things to the government. It could be a spotted owl, a red cockatoo woodpecker, wetlands, a watershed, noise; it could be a lot of things. For some reason, the government figures it's better not to use that land for what I had wanted. Instead, they want to fix it to where it could only be one house over two acres. Well, that probably cuts the value of my property at least in half. The theory is that if I build apartments and there's too much development, that it would put too much strain on the environment.

The government rezones it and that takes my right away to use it for what I wanted. I can't understand that. We don't want dirty drinking water. We're not out to ruin the environment. But then the government will decide all of a sudden that if they want to build something I wanted to build, then my land would be a good place to build it because the land is cheap.

Well, the land is cheap because they wouldn't let me build what I wanted on it. I don't think people understand that point. I could give a bunch of examples of times when they've taken the owner's rights away and then used that cheap land to build something. I could talk about it all day. When you go to public hearings, you'd be surprised how many people think that's a good way to do. Maybe it clears their conscience to take other people's money because they're so selfish.

They're not real picky about taking people's land away. I want to be sure to talk about the school board taking my land up on Lead Mine Road. I had to go to court to get my money out of them and they were just not very honest. When I started building Greystone, which was a big five hundred acre planned development, one of the things I wanted there was a school. We were also going to have a daycare and other things. I gave the school board an option over a certain period of time to build a school. I thought it would make the community complete. The option ran out and they hadn't exercised it.

They decided to break the law and try to figure out a way to keep the land when they hadn't done their work on time. I'll never forget meeting with the school board and what the judge said about the way that the government did business. He told the chairman of the school board that he couldn't believe they'd treat anyone like they treated me by trying to steal my land when the option ran out. The truth is that they were just too slow and slack to get it done in time. The judge said, "How do you expect to ever get any other developers to cooperate with you when you act like this?"

The answer was typical government. He said, "We were hoping Mr. Ammons wouldn't tell any of the others."

I can't imagine anything worse than that in the world. I don't know any level of government that I have very much respect for.

Not too long ago, someone faxed me a story that sums up quite a few of the problems we've had with the government. It's exaggerated, of course, but it makes a good point.

It starts when the Lord speaks to Noah and says, "Noah, in six months I am going to make it rain until the whole world is covered with water and all the evil things are destroyed. But, I want to save a few good people and two of every living thing on the planet. I am ordering you to build an ark." In a flash of lightning, He delivered the specifications for the ark.

"OK," Noah said, trembling with fear and fumbling with the blueprints, "I'm your man."

"In six months it's going to start raining," the Lord said. "You better have my ark completed or learn to swim for a long, long time!"

Six months passed, the sky began to cloud over, and the rain began to fall in torrents. The Lord looked down and saw Noah sitting in his yard, weeping. There was no ark.

"Noah!" shouted the Lord. "Where is my ark?" A lightning bolt crashed to the ground right beside Noah.

"Lord, please forgive me," begged Noah. "I did my best, but there were some big problems. First, I had to get a building permit for the ark's construction, but your plans did not meet their code. So, I had to hire an engineer to redo the plans. But then I got into an argument with him about whether to include a fire-sprinkler system.

"My neighbors objected, claiming that I was violating zoning ordinances by building the ark in my front yard, so I had to get a variance from the city planning commission.

"Then, I had a big problem getting enough wood for the ark because there was a ban on cutting trees in order to save the spotted owl. I tried to convince the environmentalists and the Fish and Wildlife Service that I needed the wood to save the owls, but they wouldn't let me catch them, so no owls.

"Next, I started gathering up the animals, but I got sued by an animal rights group that objected to me taking along only two of each kind.

"Just when the suit was dismissed, the EPA notified me that I couldn't complete the ark without filing an environmental impact statement on your proposed flood. They didn't take kindly to the idea that they had no jurisdiction over the conduct of a Supreme Being.

"Then, the Corps of Engineers wanted a map of the proposed flood plan. I sent them a globe.

"Right now, I'm still trying to resolve a complaint with the Equal Opportunities Commission over how many minorities I'm supposed to hire.

"The IRS has seized all my assets claiming that I am trying to leave the country, and I just got a notice from the state that I owe some kind of use tax. Really, I don't think I can finish the ark in less than five years."

With that, the sky cleared, the sun began to shine, and a rainbow arched across the sky. Noah looked up and smiled. "You mean you are not going to destroy the world?" he asked hopefully.

"No," said the Lord. "The government already has."

Chapter 7

Overcoming Avalon

When I started Greystone, my plans had always been to have a mixed-use development. This means a development with different types of houses, recreational facilities, offices, shopping, and other things. One of the things we really wanted in the area was an elementary school. We had previously worked with the school board on another elementary school and we thought it was a very nice addition to any neighborhood. So, we made a deal with the school board that allowed us to sell them some land at a favorable price in order to build an elementary school. However, we wanted to make sure that the land was used to build a school. There was a provision to the sale that if the school wasn't built in a certain amount of time, we would get our land back. We didn't want them to sell our land to someone else. We wanted a school.

Just as the time was expiring, they still hadn't built the school. We found out that the school board and school superintendent had deceived us by making up meeting minutes after the fact in order to meet the deadline. That's not right. It was very clear that they had messed around and not done their part for our agreement. To get around it, they falsified records that made it look like they were doing the right thing.

Later, we went to court and won damages from them. We were still able to work out a deal for them to build a school on the property. I kept wondering after what they had done how they were supposed to be the leader of all the schools. What were they passing along to the students? They expected their teachers to talk about telling the truth and treating others as you would want to be treated. They did not set a very good example.

I had planned for Greystone, a five hundred acre planned community, to have a mixed-use development. We were fortunate enough to get a five hundred acre tract of land right at the city limits of north Raleigh in the fastest growing part of town. I don't know how we lucked into it. I guess God gave it to us or something. But we took it as a very important responsibility. Friends of mine would tell me that people from the bank and others were talking about going out with me and looking at the land. They'd say, "Old Jud was out there riding us around in his Jeep in the woods waving his arms talking about what he was going to do."

That was the truth. I did do that. It was so easy to picture things—a lake over here, a lake over there, a road around the lake, a daycare over there, church sites, a school, shopping, offices, retirement living, and so forth. It was a chance to try to put together many of the things I had dreamed about. *It was an opportunity to quit dreaming and actually do something, and many people don't take that chance.*

We were able to work with the city of Raleigh. They've always been very easy to work with. We wanted to use quite a few greenways, and it so happened that at that time Raleigh was getting fairly well known for having a far-reaching greenway program. I was really into it. We didn't want neighborhoods to back right up to each other. I've always thought that people don't mind living a little closer together as long as between each forty houses or so there's a more wooded area that groups them together. That's the way that we built Greystone and people seemed to like it. We also were one of, if not the first, developer to use models to such a large extent in selling homes. We were continually looking for ways to make it a better area.

In a dream world, you'd never have to drive a car. You could walk or ride a bike to your workplace and to all the shopping you would need. In reality, that can't happen unless you require people to work in the area they live. Obviously, that's not going to happen. But we tried to peck away at it. We wanted people to be able to go to the pool without driving or go to some shops without driving. Greystone was our first chance to implement some of the things we had always talked about.

One of the other things we had always wanted to have was something for retirement or the elderly. We were just getting started when a group in Raleigh known as The Lightfoot Group contacted me. They had about thirty or thirty-five people. They weren't old people; they just had in mind building something that would be entirely for retirement-type living. Since I was doing Greystone, members of that group contacted me and we talked about it. One thing led to another and finally I met with the group. We even went on a tour up to Virginia near Busch Gardens to see some housing that might suit them.

It became pretty clear as we were meeting with them that it was going to be very hard to design something that was going to make a group of thirty to thirty-five people happy. You know what they say about anything designed by a committee. It seemed to be a better idea to think about it in the back of our heads and come up with our own plan and then let whoever wanted to buy in buy in. The other way was doing it backwards.

Several other things were happening at this same time. One of them was that a group got together at First Baptist Church in Raleigh, where I went to church. We talked about some sort of housing for the elderly. I had a lot of interest in it.

Along about that time, my grandmother, who still lived up in the mountains, had planned to go to a Baptist retirement home. It was a church-sponsored home in North Carolina. She had heard it talked about in her church all the time she had gone there. Her husband had been a Baptist minister all his life—this was the man I used to tag along with when he went visiting—and she remembered taking up offerings to support people that moved there.

But when the time came for her to actually go, they had all these reasons why they couldn't take her. They said she might wander off and all these other things. I thought that was one of the sorriest deals I've ever been a part of. If it wasn't built for people like her, then who? Were they waiting for elderly people in perfect health that presented absolutely no risk? If they were, I bet it was a long wait.

That made me start thinking more seriously about what I wanted to build. I knew how to do the building, but I certainly didn't know how to do everything. About that time, I met with Marshall Evans, who went to First Baptist Church with me. He worked with the Public Health Service, which meant he knew about dealing with the government, and he knew something about health care and nursing homes. I asked him if he thought it would be possible to build a life care center, and he said he thought it was. I also asked him if he would be willing to run the place, and he said he would.

I decided that no matter what we did, it needed to be a combination of things. These days, they call it life care, which is a place where you can have an apartment or house and nursing home and assisted living all in the same place. That means as the needs of people change, they can be met at the same place. There are a lot of services and amenities that are needed, such as food service, gardens, a bank, stores, a beauty parlor, a library, pool, and social activities.

Shortly after I had first talked to Marshall, we took a trip with our wives to the Grand Ole Opry in Nashville, Tennessee. We were riding along and talking about it. Marshall said he knew all about the business and how to organize things. I said, "That's what we're going to do. When we get back, we're going to build us a place."

This turned out to be Springmoor, a total life care center for over six hundred residents. In the meantime, some other things happened. Other people were able to get involved. One of them was Mary Louise Stewart, who we later named our health center after along with her husband, Dan, who is on our board and still lives at Springmoor. She was active in a lot of things in Raleigh, including the Raleigh Woman's Club. She was really caught up with the idea of building a life care retirement community, as we call it now. We felt it filled the needs of people I knew at my church and even people like my grandmother. It also fulfilled the needs of The Lightfoot Group. It was another service that we could provide at Greystone. We had ideas of a daycare being there and elderly people from Springmoor could work there. Although everything we envisioned didn't work out, it sounded like a good idea. Everything seemed to be coming together.

I asked Marshall to tell part of the story about how Springmoor came about, because he was very closely involved in it.

> *"About this time in the early 1980s, it seemed that several groups were going to build a life care center in the Raleigh area. The Episcopal Church, a Methodist group, and several private individuals and developers had undertaken feasibility studies, sought publicity, and generally stirred up a lot of interest. A place called Avalon had gotten underway and failed. It was important to us that we keep quiet about our plans until we*

were sure that we were going to do it and could obtain the necessary financing."

Marshall is right. I wanted us to gain credibility by working, not talking. But first, we wanted to put together some idea of what we wanted to do. Along with my wife and some other people, we visited places similar to what we had in mind. There weren't many to visit, but we tried to get some ideas about what to do. It's not like today, where there's a retirement community on every corner.

As those ideas were beginning to take shape, Mrs. Stewart was putting together a list of people that she knew in Raleigh. The list had about forty to fifty people on it. It wasn't just people that were interested. These were people who wanted to know when they could pay their deposit. I thought, "Now we're really getting somewhere."

Then we put together some ideas of what it might look like. It changed a lot, but it was a start. We had a meeting at the Marriott with some of the people from Mrs. Stewart's list and people from our church and others. We placed an advertisement in the local newspaper, *The News and Observer*, which also helped generate attendance.

Three hundred to four hundred people were invited and even more than that showed up. They didn't show up to talk. They wanted to know when they could move in. They didn't want to listen to a presentation; they wanted to know who they were supposed to make the check to. We were really moving along. At first, we had been anxious, because we didn't know if the main reason for the attendance was just curiosity, a genuine interest, or simply a free meal. That meeting helped us see the possibilities. People seemed very interested. One woman brought a check for $200 and wanted to "get on the wagon." She came to live at Springmoor and still resides there at the Stewart Health Center.

"As a loosely-formed group, each of us began exploring our options and gathering information we thought we would need," Marshall recalls. *"We visited Carol Woods in Chapel Hill on several occasions. They enjoyed a reputation as a highly successful life care community, and they were the 'model' for this area of the state. Our most helpful visit was to Lakewood Manor, a Baptist-affiliated life care community in Richmond, Virginia. The administrator, Albert Sims, was a Baptist minister that grew up in Raleigh. He and his staff opened their doors to us and shared many of their experiences in program planning, financing, marketing, and staffing. They shared not only their successes, but also their failures, so that we might avoid some of those pitfalls. When our marketing got underway, Mr. Sims agreed for us to bring a few prospective residents to visit Lakewood Manor so they could see a life care community in action."*

We had to figure out how we were going to finance and structure our community. That led to talking to our accountant, James A. Lucas, Sr. Then we got involved with Jim Seay, an attorney in Raleigh who was sort of the spokesman for The Lightfoot Group. As it turned out through the years, Jim Seay and his assistant, Myrtice, have come to be some of our very best friends. He and his assistant do all of our legal work, and it all started with Springmoor. Jim had a lot of interest in it and had good credibility with other people. He helped us form a group that included Ivie Clayton, the former Commissioner of Revenue who also attended First Baptist. Once we got our group together, we had to figure out how we were going to structure it.

They wanted it to be a non-profit organization, and I didn't like that word. Non-profit implies that you're not making money and even losing money, and you can't lose money and stay in business. But we came up with a structure where Springmoor itself was non-profit and a for-profit group owned the land and buildings and stuff.

Then, we had to figure out how we were going to raise money. We put together a little booklet that talked about "The Heritage," which is what we were going to call it. However, we soon learned that using that name might be confused with the name being used by Jim Baker, a television evangelist based near Charlotte. While church affiliation played a major part and provided a lot of impetus, we certainly didn't want any affiliation like that. No one can really remember where the Springmoor name was created. Marshall says that he first heard it from my wife and I, but we don't remember where it came from.

> *"While she held no official position on the staff or Board of Directors, Jo Ellen's contribution to Springmoor was very important," Marshall says. "She participated in decision making at all levels, visited communities to learn all she could about life care, offered large doses of enthusiasm and encouragement when we hit snags or became discouraged, and contributed in a major way to the presentation of the life care community through design considerations, continuity of space, and decorating. She has exceptional ability in seeing problems while they are small and advocating steps to deal with them. She was instrumental in identifying several people who became key members of the Springmoor staff.*
>
> *"I remember fondly that one day that spring, she fixed a picnic lunch and loaded the car complete with card table and chairs. Jud and I*

went to the site where trees were being cleared and spent several hours enjoying delicious food, thinking, planning, talking, and dreaming. Jo Ellen just has a special touch and instinct for interpersonal relations."

What many people don't realize is that my wife has never been on the payroll at Springmoor. She spends many hours each day updating the surroundings, decorating interiors, and making new residents feel comfortable. But she does it all without any compensation. People might say, "Well, she's your wife, she's expected to do that." I don't think so. She goes above and beyond the call of duty just about every single day.

We went around to different banks trying to find financing for the project, and although the banks were friendly and nice, at least five or six turned us down. They had never heard of doing anything like this, because life care was a relatively new term. Even worse than that, I had never done one. No one in our group had done one. This was lots of money we were talking about—in the millions and millions of dollars. It wasn't a small project. With all those variables coming together, it looked like nobody wanted to help us too much.

The government did have a system where you could go to the state and get what they called revenue bonds, or some type of tax-exempt bonds. They were intended to help finance places similar to what Springmoor was designed to be. It had to be strictly non-profit organizations, so it had been used for hospitals and things like that.

We considered going that route, but we discovered there were a lot of reasons why it was bad to go that way. You had to pay a lot of accountants and lawyers to draw up things like a prospectus, and it wound up costing close to six or eight cents or more on the dollar. I'd call that throwing money down a rat hole. The plans have to be more complete and there has to be a bidding process. There are just a lot of rules around it. The way they had it set up, our costs probably would have gone up twenty or thirty percent. So not only do you have to pay more, it takes longer and makes it harder to do. It also takes money away from the state treasurer, because by making them tax-free bonds it means that whoever has the bonds doesn't have to pay any money on the interest that they make.

The government isn't really interested in helping people. It's interested in controlling people's lives. If the revenue bonds were as good a deal as they said, then why did they have to throw in a provision that you'd not only be tax-exempt, you'd also get out of paying property taxes? We have a weak system that has to be propped up by another weak system.

That may not make sense to some people, but if tax-exempt revenue bonds are already such a good deal, then that's one break that they're supposedly giving people. To make sure they'd work, they had to give another break, which is not paying property taxes. That means the state and federal government are losing money on bond interest and they're losing property taxes. We're not quite so lucky. Since Springmoor has been open, we've paid enough into their coffers to pay entirely for the new elementary school they built up the road from us. I hope the kids are getting a good education over there, because we've paid for the whole thing. It just doesn't make sense. If I'm a for-profit corporation, then there's no way that I should be able to give you more for your dollar than a government-supported business. But it happens more than people think.

The bank that eventually worked with us a lot was Northwestern Bank, which also is a mortgage company. The president was George Collins, who was from North

Wilkesboro, and he could not have been a better friend. If it hadn't been for them, we wouldn't have built most of the things that we built.

I think that by being from North Wilkesboro, which is located in the mountains, they had a philosophy similar to the way we looked at things. They thought that a bank was meant to help people. To this day, I can't say enough nice things about them for helping us like that. It sure isn't the same philosophy that is held by big banks today.

Once again, Marshall Evans remembers a key point in the deal.

> *"As the bank edged ever so slowly towards a commitment, we were confronted with a sudden crisis," he recalls. "The banking officials insisted in one meeting that residents would have to subordinate their contract rights to the rights of the lending institution. Jud adamantly refused. He stated that anyone who put up their money to come to a life care community that he built would not be sharing in the financial risk. As I recall, he made his point by stating that if the bank required subordination of resident contract rights, the meeting was over and they could just, 'Go to hell.' At that point, the crisis evaporated."*

Once we figured out about the money, we had to figure out exactly what we wanted to build. With most appraisers, you have to figure out what will work and how you will make money doing it. Only then do you develop a workable system. That's not how we wanted to do Springmoor. We wanted to develop it based on what people wanted and needed, and I thought that I understood that because of my experience with my grandmother. Once we figured out what people needed then we wanted to work from there, instead of the other way around. Instead of reacting to the needs of the people that would be living there, we wanted to anticipate them and take care of them ahead of time.

The purpose was to come up with something that was needed. Anyone who moved there was to understand that this was their home and we were there to help them. It wasn't going to be some kind of institution. When the public thinks of a "rest home" they think bad thoughts. That's why we weren't building a "rest home."

We spent lots of time on details to make it look residential. On many occasions, that made it hard to build, especially in dealing with the insurance department and fire safety regulations. Making it look residential was not the normal way of doing these types of buildings. But we knew there had to be a way to make both ideas work.

There was no zoning category that fit what we wanted to do with Springmoor. We talked to the city about it, and no matter what I've said about the government, the city of Raleigh has always been very different from most other government agencies. We've been very fortunate to have two very good city managers. Raleigh's government has reflected the styles and attitudes that those people use to help others and make the rules more workable. With help from them, we were able to build a category for life care. It encompassed lots of other categories. That enabled us to use the land as we wanted.

We were very worried about having credibility. Avalon had already had its problems. We were just some bunch of random people. We weren't even church-affiliated. Fortunately, we had a great board of directors who worked very hard and also had a lot of credibility. We also had a good advisory board, and as we were setting it up, we wanted to include people who would help with credibility.

Mr. Dan Moore, a former governor and state Supreme Court justice then in law practice in Raleigh, was from the mountains, very near where I'm from. I always considered him one of the most credible people I knew. I went to see him one day and asked him to be on the board. He told me he was asked to be on a lot of boards and wanted to know why he should be on ours.

I said, "We need you. We know how to do the project, but we need some credibility. People don't know me from Jack, but they know you." He said that he liked honest answers, so he would be on our board. He later moved to Springmoor and his wife still lives there. It was attitudes like that that helped us get started.

When you start dealing with the elderly, you begin to realize how much they know and how much they communicate through things like the AARP. I remember one particular state that had eight or ten church-affiliated facilities go broke. When you say "church-related," people tend to think that meant the church backed the facilities. But when you get down to the business part of it, churches are good about giving facilities their blessing, but not so good about giving them their money, especially in underwriting the liability.

In dealing with the bank, the way we wanted to make sure the people who lived there didn't have liability, it didn't take us long to figure out that we could have more credibility than the church-related facilities. That doesn't mean we thought we were ahead of the church or better than the church. It's just a fact. People knew us in Raleigh. They could look at what we had done and other projects we had done. They also knew people who were involved with us, which helped our credibility. That confidence they had in us helped make Springmoor so successful.

Even though we knew it would eventually be of benefit, we operated under a handicap from the very beginning by choosing not to be church-affiliated. We went through the legislature to try and alleviate that handicap, but of course they wouldn't help. Then we went through the court system to try and get them to make it unconstitutional that the churches didn't have to pay property taxes. We won, and they said the other places had to pay two years of back property taxes. I thought we were finally all going to be on equal footing. When the court says something, the tendency is to think that you're actually going to get results from it.

But, the legislature immediately started working on a way to try to get around it by taking the word "church" out and substituting other flimsy wording that would only apply to churches. That's when I came to realize that in dealing with the legislature, you have to remember two things. First, those doing the voting knew very little about what they were voting on. Even worse, they had very little interest in learning what they were voting on.

You would think that the discussion would be about good and bad or right and wrong. But I was told by some of those in power that they had little concern for those things. They wanted to talk about movers and shakers and who had the right amount of power. Maybe the reason they don't have any interest in right or wrong is because that's not how they decide to vote. Most of them decide based on what the party leaders or committee chairmen tell them to do. They just want to get reelected or get a more powerful job. It's a waste of time to learn about the issues, because they've already been told what to do.

People might say that's too harsh, but that's exactly what my experience has been. The end result of all this is that the fifteen or twenty percent of people in North Carolina that don't live in church-related facilities have to pay a lot of fees that other people don't.

One time, I had told one of the patriarch preachers involved in the Presbyterian facility in this area how unfair the situation was. He wrote me a letter that said he thought I should have enough political clout to look out for myself.

I guess the churches themselves don't even care about right and wrong when money is involved. I still have that letter. I like to use it to remind myself that often the people you wouldn't expect are only looking out for themselves. As usual, if you follow the money trail the answer will appear.

• • •

Marshall did a lot to help train David to take over at Springmoor. But David got involved even earlier than that. Three or four months before he got out of college, we were starting to get a little worried about the marketing effort. It had begun going great guns, but it was slowing up a little. We had even gone up to the Washington area to hire a marketing firm to get back on track. After having them on the job, we finally realized that mainly what they were doing was talking a lot. The sales were nearly zero.

David was thinking about what he wanted to do and he decided to come to Springmoor. We cut the contract with the marketing people and gave him the job of marketing director. He knew how bad we wanted it and that made all the difference. He knew that I had signed enough loans that if things went bad, the money was coming out of my hide. Within six months time, our marketing was back going great guns and it hasn't slowed up since. Once again, having a desire to get something done prevails. Those marketing people were mainly interested in flying down and eating a big fancy meal at our expense.

Marshall remembers some of the problems we had getting started:

> *"As Springmoor occupancy and operation got underway, it soon became apparent that the organization's cash flow would not be adequate to cover operating expenses, lease payments, and bank debt service. Jim Seay, Jud, Mason Williams, and I deliberated over several months on*

alternatives to assure the financial stability of Springmoor. One option was to increase monthly fees, which we considered unfair. This was ruled out, and such an increase would have to be significant. That could affect our credibility, which was one of our main issues, and also adversely affect marketing. We were confident that the negative cash flow would lessen over time, as turnover increased and entrance fees increased with inflation. We were also hopeful that interest rates, which were quite high at the time, would come down, thereby decreasing the debt service payments.

"To assure the immediate and long term financial stability of Springmoor, we developed a cooperative 'Action Plan' under which Ammons Springmoor Associates and Ammons, Inc. would defer lease payments on buildings when the cash flow was not sufficient to meet leases and debt service. This major financial sacrifice on the part of the owners of the property assured the financial stability of the community, assured adequate reserves to meet unexpected financial demands, and assured that monthly fees would not increase more than the cost of living. That plan is still in effect as of this writing.

"In planning for Springmoor, development of operating policy and procedures and accounting systems were a challenge. Basic structure was put into place very early in the planning stages. The structure was expanded and refined over the first few years, and today Springmoor has one of the most responsive accounting systems, operating procedures, and resident policy manuals to be found in the industry.

"One very important objective in the Springmoor development was to have a comprehensive life care program and health care plan to meet the needs of residents. The area of health care was the greatest challenge. We had already planned an on-site inpatient care center for custodial and nursing care. We decided that the best way to meet a goal of daily living of residents was to have a care level somewhere between independent residence in homes and inpatient care. Springmoor's supportive living was conceived to meet this need.

"The Center was designed to provide independent residence in small apartments with increased services to assist those people who needed some help but didn't yet require inpatient care. It provides three meals a day, has activities and entertainment designed for those with limitations, and has an on-site nurse to provide intermittent help geared to the individual needs of each resident. Even though people might have physical limitations, the Congregate Center allowed them to remain virtually independent.

"We also planned a comprehensive outpatient clinic. The outpatient plan called for nurses to make 'house calls' to give assistance and to monitor those that were temporarily ill. The clinic design included medical care examining rooms, space for a dentist, and other health care providers. It has proven to be an invaluable service to residents and to the image of Springmoor. When we started, the clinic was planned to have 100 beds. A combination of two forces soon made it apparent that that size was inadequate. First, a professional staff had to be on hand with the

opening of the health center to meet regulatory requirements and the anticipated needs of residents. However, initially there were few patients. To meet the staffing expense, Springmoor accepted residents directly into patient care at the custodial level. At that time, state health care regulations did not prevent that practice. Secondly, the care of patients at the clinic has always been exceptional, so long term care is longer on the average than is found in the industry, since the patients are living longer.

"When it was apparent that the health center would require expansion to provide additional beds, Springmoor was one of the first to provide specifically designed space, staff, and a program of care for those residents with Alzheimer's disease and with other forms of dementia. This special care program was another way we tried to promote the independence of residents. This special wing was named in honor of Jim Seay, a primary visionary in the planning and development of Springmoor.

"In the last couple of years, more beds were added to the clinic—the Stewart Health Center— to meet the growing inpatient demand and also to provide specially designed private rooms, which residents indicated they preferred. The Board of Directors named the addition in honor of Ivie Clayton, another strong supporter of the project who served on the Board since the beginning of the planning stages.

"Much effort went into deciding which services Springmoor would staff to provide and which services would be contracted. We contracted food service and health care providers rather than have 'company doctors.' Initially, we

staffed for grounds maintenance but changed to contract service after a couple of years. After much consideration, we decided to allow residents to use doctors of their choice rather than specified medical care providers. That acknowledged the importance of the doctor-patient relationship and freedom of choice in medical care, and it ran contrary to the plans of other life care communities in the early 1980s. We also entered into contracts with designated health care providers that came to Springmoor and provided care in the outpatient clinic.

"For convenience and as a sign of their confidence in these physicians, the majority of residents have chosen our contract physicians for their primary medical care. However, from the outset we have provided transportation for those who use off-site providers. We also wanted to protect our residents from the adverse cost of continuing medical care, and the initial plan provides that Springmoor will pay all medical costs covered by the Medicare program that is not paid by Medicare or insurance providers. This form of insurance was unique to Springmoor in 1983.

"The paperwork associated with dealing with Medicare and health insurance was a frustrating job from the outset. To meet this need, we established an insurance department to handle all administrative paperwork. Residents generally perceive this to be one of Springmoor's most important services.

"That was just the tip of the iceberg when dealing with the government. Different requirements, from zoning to food service *regulations, were encountered nearly every day. Perhaps the most illustrative of these requirements was what I ran into when dealing with the health care center. Our architect and I worked very closely with the N.C. Division of Facility Services in every phase of planning. We thought we met their conditions in every way possible, and we were assured that we were in compliance.*

"Then, I got the shock of my life. A staff member of Facility Services determined that we could not be licensed to operate the health care center because we had not met some obscure requirement. It was rather inconvenient timing, considering that people had paid their money and were on the way. We produced documentation that showed the close work we had done with Facility Services to meet all the requirements, but the obstacle remained. As a last resort, Jud met with the director of the Division of Facility Services. Within a few days, we received a brief letter stating that 'in the interests of equity,' we would receive a license.

"In the fall of 1983, other residents began moving into the first phase of apartments, homes, and villas. The health center was not yet completed, the kitchen was still under construction, and our activity space was not yet ready. To meet the food service needs, we provided only the evening meal, which was served through a contract with Baxleys, a well-known caterer in Raleigh owned by Bert Brown, Jud's former college roommate and best friend.

"The early residents were understanding and in good spirits, but they must have looked forward to the days when full service would be provided. To

meet health care needs of those early residents, we established an 'outpatient clinic' in the guest rooms located in the first phase of the east apartments. The nurses and other staff were very dedicated in looking after needs of early residents. The first couple of years were a continuing challenge, as we operated a life care community in the midst of a construction site."

One thing that stuck out to me was the way people that moved in at Springmoor acted. I knew people from the business world that were as tough and ruthless as you would believe. But the people that moved in were so very nice. I guess it's a little disappointing to me that I was surprised that people could be so nice, but that was such a pleasant surprise at the time. I couldn't decide if it was that the generation that was retirement age was just plain nicer than other generations, or if everyone gets nicer as they get older. My wife thinks that as you get older you get nicer, so she says there's still some hope for me to turn out nice.

You could learn so much from our residents. They came from all different walks of life. They were so happy living an independent lifestyle in a setting that gave them some security. Seldom did you have a resident that was tough to deal with, but we did occasionally have a family member that was difficult. It always seemed to be a family member that wasn't very close to the person we had as a resident. They wanted to be a hero, even though they didn't come visit a lot. The people who were there a lot were able to see that their loved one was in good hands.

We had one woman who had her mother there, and her mother had an accident on the stairway. It was unavoidable, but it happened. The daughter just went bananas about what we had to do for her to make things right. She said she was going to sue. We didn't want to pay anything because we didn't think we had done anything wrong. But our insurance company wanted us to pay her a little to make her go away, so we settled. We called the daughter as soon as that was done and said, "Now that it's settled, when is your mother leaving?" She told us that she wasn't going to be leaving, because she liked it at Springmoor.

We said, "You said you loved your mother and you told everybody how bad we were. We just knew that as nice as you are, you would never want to leave your mother in such a bad situation." She told us that she liked it there and she got good service. I guess that leads you to the unavoidable conclusion that it wasn't about her mother. It was about money.

• • •

Marshall was starting to think like me when it came to the government.

> "During every phase in planning, developing, and operating Springmoor, it would be almost impossible to adequately describe the investment of time, energy, cost, and frustration in dealing with government requirements. Construction procedures, food service regulations, and medical health care rules are faced at every turn. The interpretation of such restrictions by regulators only compounded the problem. Perhaps the administration of guidelines is the only opportunity in their lifetime to 'flex their muscle' and impose their will."

We worked so hard to make sure we had credibility and that everyone's money was safe. We built the buildings and the campus, and people were starting to come and check us out. They'd have their lawyer or accountant investigate things for them. We were filled to capacity and everyone seemed happy. Along about then, the state decided it was time for the insurance department to start regulating people like us. They'd never changed a bedpan, invested any of their money, or taken someone's application. They weren't planning on doing anything even if we were bad, except maybe tell people we were bad. They weren't going to give people back their money if we took it from them illegally or something.

But here they came anyway. They had list after list, making these quarterly reports to fulfill some crazy desire to try and regulate us. They're still doing it. We still spend time and money complying with them. I haven't figured to this day how they think it's possible for them to be of service to anyone.

We welcome any potential residents and the questions they might have, but the government thinks it would be more beneficial for them to come in and ask the questions about whether or not we know how to make it financially sound. Why does the government care? Do they want to live there? If we're bad, eventually word is going to get around and we'll have to go out of business. In a free enterprise system, which I still like to hope exists in America, you're not going to last long if you do bad business.

However, for all of those involved in developing Springmoor, I'm sure nothing will ever mean as much to us as everything that went along with developing that project. Meeting the needs of over six hundred elderly residents is really a labor of love. It's not like building apartments, where the goal is to make money. It's something you do because you want to.

We're starting to see other people getting in the business because they think it's a surefire way to make money. It's not. It's something you do because you want to help people. It gets to the point where you like the people who live there and they become your friends. It won't be long before I live there myself. I'm sure we won't ever do anything that will mean as much to us as Springmoor.

Chapter 8
A Big Pile of Sand and
A Lot of Opportunity

One day back in the mid-80s, a man from one of the savings and loans called me and wanted to know if I wanted to go to the Outer Banks of North Carolina and look at some land they owned down there. I said I sure would, so Mr. Jim Seay, my good friend and confidante through the years, and I rode down there with the guy from the bank. We looked around and it was the first time I'd ever been there. There were lots of sand dunes and the land

they had went from the ocean to the sound. The only thing on their land, which was about four hundred acres, was the Nags Head town hall and the water tank. Other than that, it was vacant property right in the middle of the fastest growing area in the state.

I remember I spent a couple of hours walking by myself on the beach and by the sound. A thousand things flashed through my head about what we could do there in the way of development. Later on, somebody asked me why I decided to do anything at Nags Head. I told them I had never tried to build anything on a pile of sand before. That was so true. It was just big piles of sand. I thought it would be a great place to work. I had worked at the mountains and other places, but this was something totally new and different. I saw it as a challenge.

Coming home, we started talking price with the banker. There were three of us, so one had to be in the back seat. But the banker got in the back seat with me and we got out a yellow legal pad. About two hours later, Jim Seay asked us what we were mumbling about. I told him we had just finished our deal. We had it written on the yellow pad. We had it figured out how I was going to buy the land and they were going to help us with the money and we were going to develop it. When two people want to work out something, they can usually find a way to do it.

They'd had the land for a few years and tried to develop some of it, but that wasn't their expertise. We talked about it and decided we needed a golf course and some other things and made a deal. We were ready to start soon after that.

The first thing we felt we had to do was go through the town of Nags Head and get our plans approved. They didn't have what we called a Planned Unit Development ordinance. This type of ordinance means you wouldn't zone all four hundred acres separately. Rather, you'd put it all in one pot and decide what the best uses were to make a total community. Since they didn't have an ordinance like this, we had to help them write one. You always have some opposition if you want to do something new or different, but we decided the best way to do it would be to put the town commissioners in my van and ride up to Raleigh. We went around in my van and looked at some things we had done that would be similar to the type of community we wanted to build at Nags Head.

I told them if they liked what we had done, they should approve my plan. If they didn't like it, then they shouldn't approve my plan, and maybe somebody would come along and buy the land and do a better job than I would do. They seemed to like what they saw that I had done in Raleigh, so we developed a plan with them. They had a lot of input. They were a nice bunch.

The mayor was a retired Air Force man and I thought he was the nicest gentleman. He was big into CAMA, the Coastal Area Management Act, which was intended to protect the fragile coastal environment. He was into all kinds of things that were supposed to protect the beaches and keep them from being overrun by people. He believed that development should be sensitive to the environmental conditions that existed at the beaches and I also believed that.

That might be surprising to some people, because they seem to think that all developers are out to destroy the environment. Nothing could be further from the truth. We work with the environment, not against it. So, I got to be very good friends with the mayor. It took a lot of debating to get everything ironed out, because it was an educational process to get both sides filled in on what was required.

After three or four meetings from morning to midnight, one guy asked me why I was getting restless. I told him, "When I got up this morning, I was staying at a hotel near here. I was on the fourth floor, which was the top, and I looked up and down the beach. The prettiest thing I could see wasn't as pretty as the ugliest thing I've ever built. I don't know why you keep getting on my case, because

what I build is going to be better than what you are used
to."

He said I was right and they approved it right then.

Since we thought we were approved, as soon as the
meeting was over, a bunch of us left and went up the beach
until we found an ice cream parlor. We all ordered a banana
split to celebrate. The next day, we found out that after we
had left the meeting at midnight, they unapproved us
because of some technicality. We had to go back again to get
final approval. Eventually, when it was approved, it was
known as the Village of Nags Head.

I think there's too much red tape. One example is that
by the time we were finished with the ten- or twelve-month
approval process and completed the first house in the
development, we had fifty-three major permits or
inspections by a government agency.

What made it so bad was that you had no idea if you
were violating anything. You didn't even know if you had
everything that you were supposed to have because there
was nobody to ask. Everyone only knows his own little
part. One time I thought we had everything that was
possible to have on God's green earth, and then somebody
came up and said we weren't finished because we didn't
have a mosquito eradication plan. What else can they add?
How would you like to be the guy that spends his whole
life focused on the mosquito eradication plan? Sounds like
a real growth industry to me. But to them, it was just as
important as if I was planning to dump big barrels of toxic
waste on the land.

One thing we wanted to do was build a golf course. I
had been to Europe and I'd heard people talking about
links courses in Scotland. I had actually built a golf course
while I was in the Air Force in France. I thought this place
was too pretty to be like everything else, so we wanted to
build a links course. We dug holes in the ground to get

water—you can't get it out of the ocean because it's too salty—and as we dug the holes it created lakes.

Now, a links course is where you preserve the surrounding environment as much as possible. We didn't just want to level the dunes to make our plan fit. We wanted to fit our plan around the dunes. We spent hours walking around and fitting the fairways and greens between the dunes.

One thing that was interesting was that we had a map showing where the dunes were, some of which were thirty or forty feet high. They were known as migrating dunes, which meant that the wind blew so much that you could have a thirty foot high dune that could move sixty feet in just a few years. They keep shifting around. Our math wasn't too good, but we had to take the shifting dunes into account. The wind blew so much that it was difficult to keep the sand still, which meant that it was easy to be off quite a bit when we were trying to prepare a seed bed. We couldn't get the beds to grow, because the dunes kept blowing around and creating rough terrain. We finally fixed the problem by putting sod on the whole course.

Another very interesting problem that arose was that the irrigation would blow off to one side. Instead of a line of sprinkler heads, we had to have two or three lines. There was a computer that judged the wind velocity and so forth and then decided which line should be used. It was a computerized system and it wound up working very well. I don't think I've ever seen a course irrigated exactly that way before.

When it opened, people seemed to really like our links course. As time went on, we were picked as a true links course and articles were written about it. Some people said we had the prettiest finishing hole on the East Coast. Of course, it was real hard not to build something pretty if you didn't mess up what was there. The ocean was on one side and the sound was on the other and there were different kinds of grasses growing. The contrast with the greens and the brown grasses and sand that were there was real pretty. Golfers seemed to really like it. It may not have been their favorite place to play every day, but when they came to the beach, they wanted a change from what they see everywhere else. They wanted to remember that they were at the beach when they played golf on their vacation.

We also started building houses and we adopted what we called the "Old Nags Head look." We wrote up specifications and rules so that they had to be followed. We wanted to use the look they'd had in Nags Head for a long time, using materials that they had used. Long ago some of their houses weren't even painted. We wanted to paint our houses, of course, but we used earth-tone colors to go with what had been there before we got there.

Our logo was a nag, which is a horse. The property we were building on had been known as a racetrack property, because in the old days, when people took the ferry across to the land, there were wild ponies out there and they would have pony races. Pirates were accused of using nags to lure ships and then loot them. The story goes that people would catch the ponies and tie a lantern around their necks. Then, they'd lead them up and down the beach to warn ships that they were in an area of treacherous coast. In fact, they called that area the "Graveyard of the Atlantic" because of all the wrecks they had there. Later on, they built the Hatteras Lighthouse in that same vicinity.

The same family had owned the land for a very long time. They were in the business of making cork and rubber gaskets. They had bought the land in the hopes that they could grow rubber trees there. They hadn't had much luck with it, though, so they decided to get rid of it. It was about four hundred acres with a mile of ocean and a mile of sound frontage. It was unheard of to find an undeveloped tract that big. That was part of the reason that we took our responsibilities so seriously. We knew we might not get another chance to do it again.

We wanted our houses to fit in and lay back in the dunes. We came up with plans to handle traffic, because you don't want to see cars parked everywhere. People came up with other ideas for the Village that we thought were real fitting, ways to create jogging trails, park trails, and other amenities.

We built beach access and a place to park with bath facilities so people could go to the beach. In two places, we gave the town some land where they could create public beach access for people who didn't live at the Village. We also built two small recreational areas and piers on the sound that were intended for families with young kids and later became a favorite spot for windsurfers.

We also built a swimming pool over near the ocean behind the sand dunes. I was so proud of that pool. We always thought, and it turned out to be true, that people go to the beach to lay near the ocean, not to go swimming. A lot of people don't want to get all salty. So, if they can have a swimming pool near the ocean, they've got the best of both worlds—clean water and an ocean view. We looked at pools in various areas and saw that usually if you built a pool near the ocean, there was a big sand dune between you and the ocean that blocked your view. To solve that, we built our pool up high on top of poured concrete and put parking under the pool. That way, we got the line of sight over the dunes and people could look over the dune at the ocean. Or, if they'd rather, we built a walkway so that you could walk down from the pool to the beach. The two were tied together.

Our trademark has always been to use mountain stone in at least part of our building. I wanted to take the stone down to Nags Head, which was going to be an expensive proposition. It's heavy and from the North Carolina mountains to Nags Head is five hundred miles.

I remember the architect saying he didn't think we should build the signs out of stone because it wasn't native to the beach. So, I asked to see his sketches. He had them made out of stucco, which is native to Venezuela. I told him, "Look, these are brown stones I'm talking about. That's the same color as sand. Sand comes from the stones." I won that argument and we built a lot of things out of that mountain stone.

We had also started another project in Wilmington a year or two before that. My oldest son, Andy, lived in Florida and worked in the construction business. I had wished he would come back and help us on many occasions, but sometimes when you're very opinionated like I am and your son is very opinionated, you're not sure how that will go over. So he was doing his thing and I was doing my thing.

One day he called his mother telling her about his trouble with labor unions and unionized employees. When he hung up, she said she thought he was about ready to come back to North Carolina. I talked to him after that and we made a deal. He moved to Wilmington, which was about four or five hours from Nags Head. He worked on two projects: Nags Head and something we were working on at Wilmington. From the time we started building the golf course on, it was Andy's project.

We built a big sewage disposal plant, which is quite a feat at the beach because the sand blows so hard and creates problems for disposal. We certainly didn't want to dump it in the sound, even though some people have been approved to do that now. Instead, we developed a system of spray beds to do it in a contained area. When we were building the golf course, you could hardly keep the sand still.

We've finished it now, and when I ride back down and look at it, it looks just as good as I had hoped. It can really make you feel good to start with something totally undeveloped and turn it into something so pretty. The steps we took to make sure we worked with the environment, not against it, wound up being worth it when I look back and see how well it turned out.

• • •

One of the big problems we had, other than the permits, was when we had just been going for two or three years and the savings and loans problem came along. Some people call it a crisis, but I wouldn't call it that.

I remember when the Resolution Trust Corporation was organized to oversee and/or take over a lot of the savings and loans. They took over one that we were doing a lot of business with, so I got a good understanding of what I thought they did. I had bought a little bit of stock in the savings and loan, and it was selling for $12 or $15 per share. We thought that was pretty good. It wasn't Microsoft, but compared to what I paid for it, I was happy. I got into the project with them developing the Village and was spending quite a bit of money. We were making some money and the S&L had already been paid a lot of money. This came along at a time in the late '80s that was a bad time for the building business.

Most people want to blame the savings and loans for the "crisis," but that's not accurate. Congress was the main one that should've gotten the blame, but of course the media would never report that. In my opinion, the whole thing got started in 1981 with the Economic Recovery Tax Act. It allowed people to write off depreciable real estate over fifteen years, and also allowed for capital gains taxation at a lesser rate than regular tax rates on the sale of real estate. It doesn't take a genius to figure out that the law was encouraging a lot of building by giving tax advantages that encouraged people to build as many things as they could.

Since so much building was going on, Congress had to loosen up on the savings and loans. After all, somebody had to be funding all this building. But then, practically overnight, the government changed their mind and passed the Tax Reform Act of 1986. It decided that people with an adjusted gross income of over $150,000 couldn't write off their real estate activity even if they had a negative cash flow, which is called passive losses. Now, who's going to buy real estate with rules like that? Nobody.

So, the savings and loans started having trouble. To make a lot of political hay out of it, the government and RTC decided that everyone in the savings and loan business was bad and the government came in and started checking it out. They had a funny way of checking, though. If they thought you had the least bit of financial difficulty, they'd send in a bunch of people and put a sign on your window that said you were bad and that they were checking on you.

Well, that did a whole lot for people's confidence. What happened then? Everybody grabbed their money out of that S&L and ran somewhere else, so then the savings and loans had even worse trouble. It wasn't anything but a scheme by the government and the bigger banks to put those S&Ls out of business. It worked, because a lot of them were gone.

After all that, of course, they had to sell out to a bigger bank, which was why the big banks liked it so much. Basically, they had to have a fire sale. But even after that they were still getting $1.50 for a share of stock. If the stock was worth anything, that meant the government lost nothing. In the beginning, the savings and loans hadn't been that bad off. But the government caused the problem. It was like that across the nation. People got hurt, people went broke, and the government and big banks orchestrated most of it.

I remember that when the RTC thought the S&L was getting to a certain place—which seemed to be a place where the government wanted to come in and tell you how to run your business—then they'd come in and run your show. One day we went down for a meeting with the S&L we did business with. There was a guy there from the RTC who did most of the talking. The RTC had been put together over a year or so, so where did they get most of the people that worked there? Well, they had been bankrupt or lost their job. These were the people who were supposedly going to tell us, who had been in doing business for twenty or thirty years, how to run our business.

We went in and the guy started talking. I've never been talked to as bad as he talked to me. He was telling me what he was going to do and what I was going to do. I said, "Wait a minute. I own it. You loaned me the money. We have an agreement."

Oh, he was sure he could get around it. They thought they could run over anybody that showed up. The meeting was real bad. I didn't know what to say. I was scared, astonished. The man went into this spiel about how he developed 10,000 lots the past two or three years in Atlanta, and how he knew more about it than anyone, and how we couldn't con him, so we should just do what he said. No agreements were going to be honored now that the RTC was there.

We just sort of listened and shuddered and then got up and walked out. Andy was with me, and he was going the opposite way, so we weren't driving together. I was really worried about him, because he was shook. He had never been around anybody like that and he was headed down to the beach to do some work. When I got home I was talking to my wife. I told her I was scared for our son to even drive a car. If you've never been there, you don't know how bad they can talk to you.

My wife decided to call him up. "Oh, no," he said. "That wasn't what my problem was. That was just the first time I've ever been in a meeting where I thought Dad was ready to give up."

I couldn't believe it. He was worried about me. They must have just overpowered me. I was sitting there with my eyes wide, like a country boy gone to town. I thought to myself, "Well, I didn't get here that way." If you want to be successful, you should never forget how you got there. So, they had told us to be back next week, they were going to have this plan, and things were going to change. They were right about one thing. Things were going to change, but not in the way that they thought. I thought, "Man, I didn't get here by being scared, so there's no reason to start now." Then I remembered my favorite saying during the bad times: Bad times don't last, but good men do.

When we got back, I said, "Y'all be real quiet. I'm going to do the talking. If you interrupt me, I'm walking out. We're not having a discussion. I came to do the talking for a few minutes and I want y'all to be quiet.

"When you told me that you had developed 10,000 lots over the past two years, you're either a liar or did such a sorry job that you got fired," I said. "If you'd done it and made any money, you wouldn't be here. So, I'm assuming you know nothing that you're talking about. I'm not scared of you anymore. I can push harder than you can push. The land is in my name now. Y'all have no choice but to deal with me and I don't want to hear anymore about it. We're not going to talk about it now. I'm walking out that door. I'll be back to talk about it next week if you invite me. I'm not coming unless you're going to have a different attitude when I come back."

Boom. I shut the door and we left.

The next week we went back and they had a completely different attitude. They acted like they wanted to be nice, but all they wanted to do was solve what they called "their problem." We didn't think they had a problem. They had made up a problem with some percentages they had pulled out of nowhere. The deal was still working, we were still making money, and the bank was even getting some money. We had never missed a day of the agreement we had.

I figured out right then that they weren't interested in good or bad. They were interested in covering their butt.

They were interested in getting something on paper to show that they had made some progress. We went back and divided up a little of the land and redid some loans. After about an hour or two we had made three or four deals. They were absolutely the easiest people to out-trade I've ever been around in my life. I thought, "How did I go from thinking they were so big and tough and smart to realizing that they don't know what they're doing?"

I came out of those meetings a lot better off than I went in. They got very little, because they didn't know how to get it. All they knew how to do was get a piece of paper signed by somebody and take it back to Atlanta and hand it to somebody and act like they were a hero. Then they could report how much the savings and loan had lost and make a lot of hay over a big political deal. They weren't interested in looking after the money. They were interested in talking about who did look after the money.

With all this happening with the banks and the RTC coming in, that was affecting our credibility some. Things were slowed up anyway and although the recession was worse in the Northeast than down where we were, eighty percent of our sales in Nags Head came from Virginia northwards. Some of those areas were hit and that decreased our buyers. Plus, the RTC was in there closing down our S&L. It seemed like everything was happening at once.

When we look back on it, it sure seems like there were a lot of complications. But those don't seem so bad when we see how well the project turned out. We went into it with a lot of responsibilities to the environment and the surrounding areas, and some people didn't think we'd be able to do a very good job with it. But we survived it all real well and finished the project. We're proud of how pretty it is, how environmentally sensitive it is, and what we learned doing it.

Chapter 9

No Wetlands, No Seafood; No Development, No Economy

Fourteen or fifteen years ago I met a person from Wilmington who had seven hundred or eight hundred acres of land just north of Wilmington. We thought that was a booming place, because it was a seaport town, and Interstate 40, which adjoined the property, was getting ready to open up down there. We thought it was a very promising situation.

We decided to seriously think about developing that land. We wound up buying it. We worked up a plan where we could build lakes and use the dirt to build roads, and then the lakes could separate neighborhoods. With that many acres, it's nice to have the neighborhoods separated so that you can have different styles and sizes of houses. The highway also divided the property. One side of the land joined Interstate 40, and we wanted to develop that into some industrial land for businesses.

As usual, the government was our biggest problem in getting the land developed. We got a letter from them telling us that they did a survey. They said I couldn't use three-fourths of what I bought and that the land was virtually theirs. That's six hundred acres that they wanted me to give away for free. They told me how maybe I could contact a couple of conservation groups or people I could give it to so I wouldn't have to pay taxes on it. It gets your attention real fast when the government starts talking about giving away six hundred acres of your land. So, I got really deeply involved in a hurry with the whole wetlands issue. I found out that what the law said and what people were trying to enforce had nothing to do with each other.

One time, Charles Kuralt came down to Wilmington to do a story. I thought he was good at the time, because he had a good reputation and was from North Carolina. I was looking forward to having him come. He and his bunch of television people came in and spent a day at our place. They only told us the day before that they were coming. We had to do all this stuff to get ready for them—take off work, bring sandwiches, all this. Very demanding bunch. But we did it, and Andy, who was in charge of the Wilmington project, went with them and tried to be very cooperative.

They filmed for about half a day. We figured the program was going to be thirty minutes long and they'd want to do some on the other groups that did not advocate development and wanted to call everything a wetland. If they did half on us and half on them, we thought we might get eight or ten minutes out of it. That wouldn't be too bad. We seemed to get along pretty well while they were doing it.

I remember the one part they liked so much. My son was standing with them and they were looking at a house we were building. There was a string going beside the house. They said, "What's that string for?" We told them it was separating the unusable wetlands—as defined by the Corps of Engineers—from the lot where we were building the house.

The television man said, "Well, I can't tell the difference, and I've looked." That was our whole point. We couldn't tell any difference between the land we could develop and the wetlands either. I thought that would be a very good point to make on TV. That's when I was naive enough to think that it would show up on the program.

When the program finally aired, there was about eighteen or nineteen minutes of this loud lady screaming and hollering and riding in a boat and talking about how her sons couldn't sell oysters anymore because of developers and others like us screwing up the water. Then there was about twenty seconds on us, which had nothing to do with us except for a statement talking bad about us. They call that reporting. I'm sure they won a lot of awards. It was a disgrace. I now think Kuralt and his show were a farce. It had very little to do with the truth. It was mainly set up to get his point across, not to tell it like it was. Among other things, it helped shape my opinion about the news media.

Often in my dealings with the news media they have reported things I thought were far from the truth. When I go to church on Sunday, people will tell me what they've read in the paper. I always figured I'd rather make the news than read the news, but apparently a lot of people would rather read it. When they read it, they take it as the gospel. Then they start talking to me about it and they just can't believe how often it's wrong or gives the wrong impression. They've given people the idea by using pictures that a wetland is where you can see water and grasses and fish. They say that destroying that type of land would be bad. Of course it would. But the truth is that wetlands very seldom look like that. Seldom does the headline, which is written for sensationalism, even match the story. But you can't fight them. It's like my dad used to tell me about the pissing contest with a skunk—you can't win.

For the next several years, it seemed like I spent much of my time arguing with the Corps of Engineers about what wetlands actually were. The definition changed pretty regularly, especially after the EPA picked up on the disagreement. Their main job is to stop anything that they can. Whether it's good or bad doesn't make a difference.

One time, I was invited to go to Morehead City to be on a panel with someone from the Corps of Engineers who ran the wetlands program and a few other people who advocated the wetlands program. I remember that panel well. Basically, it was three people ganged up against me. I think the only reason they wanted me there was to make it more interesting. This one guy, who I knew from doing business, was talking about how we shouldn't be building there. I told him I wasn't the one creating the need for houses. The Chamber of Commerce ran big ads and went looking for industry to create jobs. Those people had to live somewhere, didn't they? I happened to know that he had a son who had just gotten married and was living in town, so I said, "Where in the world is your son living? In a tree house?" I'm not even sure he got my point.

There was also a lady there who was high up in the EPA. She did a lot of her talking about how great it was to be in Morehead City and be out in the field and out where the rules were being put to use. When it was over, I went up to her and said, "You're in a convention center in Morehead City. The rules are being put to use over yonder where my land is and where you're trying to take it away from me. Why don't you get in my truck with me and take a day off and let me show you where the rules are being put to use?"

"I would love to," she said. "Mr. Ammons, I don't know anything I would rather do. But I've been gone for a week's vacation before I came down here and I've got to go back to Washington."

I was trying to be friendly, so I said, "Oh, where did you go on your vacation?"

She said, "I went down there on the Outer Banks."

"Did you really?" I asked her. "Where did you go?"

"Down there where they're building that new golf course at the place called The Village."

"Great," I said, thinking we were getting somewhere. "We're building that new golf course. How did you like it?"

She caught herself before she said something positive about development and came back with, "It's a shame what they've done to that fragile island, just a shame. All that building is going on down there and the way they've torn it up is awful."

I thought she had told me she had a good time. So I asked her, "Did you sleep in a house or did you sleep in a damn tent?"

She said, "Well, I get your point. I did sleep in a house. But they should be regulating how many people can go down there."

So, basically, she wants to make sure she gets to go and no one else gets to go. That's the typical syndrome. Roll the bridge up once I get there. Go to a meeting anywhere and the same thing happens. I've got mine; why should I let you have yours? We've started to call it NIMBY: not in my backyard.

Eighty percent of the sales we had at the coast were to people from north of the Mason-Dixon line, not North Carolinians. So I told the lady that maybe we should put a great big gate up at the bridge where everybody comes across from Virginia. The gate would keep out all the Yankees and Republicans.

She said she got my point, but she still had to go back to Washington. She wanted to go back and keep talking the same things she was talking. Everything I've done has always involved regulation. I used to think thirty years ago that I spent a lot of time working on permits and other things for the government. I probably spent twenty-five percent of my time dealing with the government and seventy-five percent working. That's changed now. *Now seventy-five percent of my time is spent on something having to do with a permit or with the government. That only leaves twenty-five percent to make money and pay taxes.*

As usual, we tried to negotiate with the county about water and sewer, and got nowhere. I told them they were wrong for not taking some of the offers we made to them about using some of their existing lines, but they thought they were too smart. Turns out that they've bought our lines now and wish they'd done it to start with and been more cooperative. It seems like if you're a developer and you offer people a good deal, they think there's something wrong with it.

It seems impossible to ever make all those government people happy. One time I thought things were going pretty good and we had done everything right. I was down at the beach near our property and picked up the Sunday newspaper one morning. There was a full-color picture of our development on the front page and a big story about a lawsuit that was being leveled against us by the Wildlife Federation, which was represented by the Environmental Defense Fund. That's not a very good way to begin a Sunday, especially when it was the first that I had heard of the lawsuit.

It was bad enough that they didn't like what I was doing, but they didn't like what the EPA or Army Corps of Engineers was giving us permits to do. We didn't even know we had a problem. They hadn't told us they were going to sue us. Apparently, that's not the way they do things.

Their fight was really with the EPA and Army Corps of Engineers. The reason they were mad with us was because we were the people doing the work that the EPA had given us permission to do. They decided to make a great example out of us and make the EPA change the rules.

We spent a lot of time making sure we were correctly interpreting the rules. We didn't even know what the rules were, but we spent our time and money trying to follow them. For doing that, we got sued because someone else thought the rules should be different.

You'd think that the Corps of Engineers would be on the same side as us. But after five minutes talking to them, we knew we were by ourselves. They didn't care what happened. They just didn't want trouble. They were willing to hang us out to dry if it meant they could get off the hook.

The way to get along with people like that is to let them think they've won something. Sometimes people say their principles can't let them do that. But every day isn't the Alamo. You can't fight the last battle of your life on every day.

We decided we'd bring a settlement to them. We had eight or nine acres that we weren't planning on using anyway. They took it as a settlement and then they made this big deal about how they'd straightened us out and now they had land that everyone could use. They acted like heroes, but they knew what had happened. We had to bite our tongues because we knew the real truth. Then they went off trying to get some more federal money and grants to go after someone else.

That's just another example of what the government thinks of private property rights. They think that those types of rights left when George Washington left.

As it turned out, we got to develop about all we wanted but not exactly like we wanted. *All their arguments cost us was that the development wasn't as pretty as it would've been without the arguments, and it wasn't as environmentally sensitive as it would've been.* They felt like heroes for hounding us. We spent more money and ended up making it worse than it would've been otherwise. Isn't that true about everything the government does?

I remember starting our industrial park in Wilmington. It was very important to get a big customer to start off, one that would have frontage on Interstate 40 and look very nice and have lots of room. There was a committee that had been working to get industry brought to Wilmington and they thought they had a few prospects. There were two prospects on Long Island and I thought it would be helpful if I personally went and visited them. I wanted to give them an idea of what we were planning and answer any questions they might have about the move. I went out to Long Island to spend the day. I wound up finding two companies that came to our industrial park. They're still there and very happy.

When I went up there, a man met me at the airport. I had never met him before, and he said to me, "Mr. Ammons, you might've wasted your time coming up here. Just across from where your land is located, some other people have an industrial park where land is cheap. I might want to go over there instead of paying you what you want for your land."

I said, "Wait a minute. You pulled up in a Mercedes-Benz with windshield wipers on the headlights. You've got on a full-length fur coat. A man like you understands quality. You haven't got any plans on going to that cheap other place. You're planning on buying from me, so let's get down to business."

He laughed, shook hands, and said I was exactly right. We made deals with him before we left that day.

Making deals wasn't always as easy as I would've liked. We've had many examples of the government trying to compete with us. They are a difficult competitor to overcome. They pay to train workers and also help pay for the water and sewer. We can't do that. We ran into that again when we were working on Northchase in Wilmington. We bought land and put up a big water tank that we wanted to put our name on. The government said that we couldn't, but the county's, which was beside of us, had the county's name on it. It was a case of living by the golden rule, because he who had the gold made the rules.

In another case, a nice company from Raleigh was moving down there. They were looking at our land, which cost $45,000 or $50,000 an acre. But they could buy some land down the road for $15,000 an acre, because it belonged to the county. In other words, the government did all the work on the land at the expense of the taxpayers and then they were able to sell it cheaply. We were paying taxes for the county to take our money and then take our business. That still happens today like crazy. People have meetings where they talk about it and make it sound like it's a good idea.

The government is funny about how they decide when they're going to compete with a private citizen. One of the biggest cases I've heard about was down at Ft. Bragg, outside of Fayetteville. They had the red cockatoo woodpecker down there. It's not as pretty as a redheaded woodpecker, and it actually looks more like a sparrow. We'd had those birds before on some of our property. When you had them, you had to mark off an area you can't touch or do other things to, so basically you lose your land. They had the same birds on some of the government land. They decided either they had to build somewhere else or they were going to run the birds off. They debated on it and decided it was in the public interest to move the birds out of there. If they had had to move, they would've had to buy other land, but if they ran the woodpeckers off, they could stay on that land and save the public's money.

It's just another example. They weren't interested in the woodpecker to start with. When it was free to be interested in the woodpecker and take my land, they liked the woodpecker. But when they had to pay to protect it, the woodpecker was no big deal.

Very seldom when you meet with the government will you be able to get the discussion on good or bad or right or wrong or fair or unfair. If that's not what the discussion is about, then why are you having it? But the government always wants to talk about their opinion or their interpretation of rule A, B, or C.

That's not the worst part of it, though. The worst thing about the government is that you can tell that they don't think things out. If you spend enough time and money, you can always get around them. If they were right and fair, you couldn't get around them that easily. You don't have to be dishonest; you just have to know that the rule wasn't really a rule to start with. So many times, the ruling you get is someone's opinion or idea of what it ought to be. More than anything, it seems like it's just a personal vendetta. It's absolutely certain that most people who are so-called environmentalists and are so up in arms about things are not growth advocates. They just tie in to some cause to stop growth.

One example is the way we were treated when we were doing the wetlands. It was very simple, because there was not really a wetlands law as such. There was one that went way, way back many years. It dealt with the marsh. Then through some hook and crook it became something else, because these people were trying to find a way to stop growth.

Then they passed this law having to do with filling. If you wanted to drain an area, such as has always been done from coast to coast, you'd dig a ditch and help water go off onto a creek or something. Over half of all farmland in Eastern North Carolina and other areas was done that way. The filling law, which had nothing to do with ditching, was passed years ago to stop the filling of valuable marshland along the coast.

They saw then that they weren't winning, because the law wasn't on their side. So they came up with all these interpretations that I called the Clod Rule. It was this dumb thing that said if you were digging a place where you were draining something and you dropped a piece of dirt off the side, then you were filling. So if the clod of dirt you dropped was over two inches, then you were breaking the law. If it came up two inches then you were filling. You could do all the ditching that you wanted to, as long as you didn't drop any over the side. So you had to have a very expensive way of doing the ditching. Basically, it was like throwing money in a rat hole. You had to spend $100,000 instead of $10,000 so that you wouldn't drop any over the side. It was a farce. But by doing that, you could get around the rule. That money could've been much better spent.

As it turned out, we had an industrial park with a number of customers, built eight hundred or nine hundred houses, and the Y took over the pool and recreation area. When you go back down there now and see how it's all built up and everything works together, it's great. Andy built all that, and I don't know how anyone could be prouder of anything than what he did. It really is a pretty place.

Chapter 10
2.75%

> *"The tax laws are revenue raisers. They were not designed to be equitable," according to a judge in the federal tax court. "They are the result of political decision that in the grand view, equity is just not helpful."*

That takes the cake. You spend all your life growing up, going to church with your mother, learning what's fair and right and wrong. As you get older, you go in the military because you want to do what's right and serve your country. Based on that experience, you think that tax laws must be based on people filing their returns and telling the truth. You think it's a very serious business not to be a crook. Then you realize that the people that are judging you aren't playing by those same rules. Their rules are mainly designed to see how much money they can collect. They'll go to any means to do all they can do to collect as much as possible. If it's not fair, that's tough. They're in favor of it.

The way the IRS operates is not fair. If a taxpayer misrepresents their income, they could wind up in jail. But if an IRS employee misrepresents the law, they can get a bonus. It's true. Auditors are rewarded based on how much additional tax they try to force people to pay. It's not based on what people actually pay; it's based on what the agent attempts to get from them. That was revealed in a 1997 *Wall Street Journal* article. Even when they impose those extra taxes, it's usually not justified. One study showed that seventy cents of each dollar that is imposed in additional taxes is unjustified.

Where does that leave the taxpayer? Where does that leave me? Do you have to take the view opposite from them? You'll do anything you can to get out of paying. When it comes time to go to church, it's a little hard to believe that, though. *My wife told me about one hundred times that if anyone else makes me act like them, then they have won.* No matter how badly they treat you, you shouldn't be as bad as they are. That leaves you behind the eight ball with the government, but you just have to suck it up. You can fight honestly, and they'll fight however they feel like it. That's how my twelve-year saga with the tax man began.

• • •

My trouble first started on July 20, 1988. We thought we reached a settlement with them in January of 1997. Two things happened, though. Way after we thought we had settled they came back without any justification trying to find something else wrong. Plus, when they first started in 1988, they can go back three years to look at your records. So, in reality the whole thing started in 1985. From 1985-1997 I dealt with the IRS. That's twelve long years. If you don't believe that they were long years, then you've never dealt with the IRS.

When my accountant, James A. Lucas, Jr., told me that the IRS auditor was coming to meet with him the first time, it didn't bother me at all. "Just give him what you've got," I told my accountant. "We don't have anything to hide. I don't care what he looks at." So, the IRS man started looking.

We should have been tipped off to start with by the fact that the guy was from some other country and barely even spoke English. That was our first problem. As a general rule, if someone is examining my financial records and has the power to throw me in jail, I want them to be speaking the same language as me.

He was mixed up from the start. He came and went through my records and then he went away for a long time; not long enough, but a long time. It was months and months. I kept hearing from people that I worked with, people that I got permits from, that he was hanging around asking for information about me. If he had just asked me for it, I would've given it to him. But he assumed that I was like him and I wasn't playing fair.

After he had been in every nook and cranny trying to get dirt on me, he showed up again. He looked my accountant in the eye and said, "We found out where Mr. Ammons is hiding his money."

My only response to that was, "I sure would like to know where it is, because I would like to go get it. I didn't even know I had lost any money."

He claimed he had checked on every deed we had filed. That was probably true, because he had a big old stack of them. There were

hundreds of deeds there. Out of those hundreds, he found four or five that were deeded to the Homeowners' Association. We gave the property referred to in those deeds to them as a donation. We didn't sell it to them. But he had gotten it mixed up with another company and he thought I was deeding property out of one company into another company. When we pointed out to him that he had been working for many months and was still screwed up, it didn't go over too well. I think it took the wind out of his sails that he thought he'd caught us being a crook, but it had turned out that he was just confused.

At that point, he told us that he wanted a lot more information because he was going to expand the audit to other companies that we had. This thing was starting to get a little bigger than we had planned on. We wanted to keep being nice, though, so we gave him all the information he wanted. Now that he had so much time invested in the whole audit without finding anything, we knew he was going to go all out on this new information we gave him. He had to find something.

After he stayed gone for a little while longer with his new information, he came back with another shocker. He said our tenants were not really who we said they were. Basically, he said we were lying about it. I guess it was getting too big for him at this point, so he had to go to Charlotte and get another man that was an authority on situations like ours. Another clue we should've gotten was that the first guy wasn't an authority on anything except speaking a foreign language.

So, those two guys set up a meeting with us. They got there late, as usual, because apparently they don't start early in their business. It was lunchtime by the time he arrived. His first visit was primarily for him to bark out orders about how much space he needed and how big his office was going to have to be and how we had to do whatever he said.

As usual, he went away and then came back again. When he came back, he announced to us that he had spent the last few years of his life trying to get Jim Baker, who ran Heritage USA and the show on TV. Baker wound up in jail over the whole thing.

He said, "I got Baker, and my last big project before I retire is going to be putting Mr. Ammons away." We hadn't given him any information at this point. That was his attitude when he walked in the door. We were all kind of in shock. We asked our friends what they thought we should do, and a few said we should go read the Constitution. At this point I didn't see how that could help us, and I thought maybe we should go read the Bible.

We thought this guy was going to be playing by some sort of rules, but he had already told us what he was going to do to us on the very first day we met him. After he announced his great big plan, he took off again. I think they have to go away for a while in order to be able to think up what they're going to say the next time that they have a meeting.

By now, it was 1989, and they decided they wanted more information from us. They wanted to refigure millions and millions of dollars worth of building that we had done. As I recall, it turned out that we were one dollar off from the reports that we had filed. It looked to us that they were making up things.

They scheduled a meeting with us at the IRS district office in Greensboro. By this time, we had hired legal counsel, because if the ship was going to go down, we wanted someone on the boat with us. Our lawyers turned out to be very good and they worked quite hard to help us.

They helped us submit all the information, and after the meeting with the district office we thought maybe we could put this thing to rest. Naturally, it didn't. The IRS came back and wanted even more information. When they got what they wanted, they decided they were going to have to send everything to Washington. We had to pay to send people up to the national office for two meetings.

Finally, in 1992 we got a letter saying that they had finally given up. We had been expecting a little longer letter. We were hoping for something along the lines of, "We're sorry," or "Sorry for all your time and trouble." Apparently, that's not the way that they work. I reckon they were just sore losers, so they just said, "Bye." They had assessed $10 million worth of penalties and got zero. Their response to that was, "Bye." I don't know about you, but when I give up on a $10 million project, I do a little more than write a short letter.

Finally, we had won something, and it was a huge win. That's if you can count winning as paying $275 an hour for attorneys to spend a bunch of hours working on the case. I guess you could say we won. They not only don't say they're sorry, they don't even pay you for all your trouble.

We thought they were backing off, but we were wrong. When you sign a lease or something there's a page or two of worthwhile information and then there's ten or fifteen pages that cover everything from motherhood to apple pie. We call that "boilerplate." They came up with all this boilerplate crap that said we owed money on about everything that anyone's ever owed money for. I read those pieces of paper and I couldn't even tell who they were talking about. So, the fight began again.

We brought in lawyers from Washington, D.C. We brought in some authorities on executive compensation and a bunch of other people. It took a lot of work to get ready for them. The burden wasn't on the IRS to prove that I was guilty. All they had to do was say I was guilty. They could just roll out of the bed, say you're guilty, and then it's up to you to defend yourself.

We kept telling them how bad their information was. All that did was make them mad. Our experts had put together a bunch of answers that were very good and would have proved to a reasonable person that we didn't owe them anything. We scheduled a big meeting that was going to be the meeting to end all meetings towards the end of 1992.

Not too far from Raleigh was a retirement business that had not done very well. They had made some mistakes in their operation, which was causing them to lose money. We thought we could buy it and turn things around by using some of our management techniques. Not only would we have helped the people that were living there, but we would also have made some money. The same day that the IRS was going to have the big meeting to talk about my companies, I went down to the retirement business and made a deal to buy the place.

On the way home, I stopped at a restaurant to celebrate the deal. While I was there, I decided to call my boys at the meeting and see how the meeting with the IRS was going. They weren't saying too much. I thought they were crying. They had gone in prepared with all their facts and figures. The IRS guy started talking and, poof, our guys shot them down. The government boys got frustrated with seeing how wrong they were, so they got mad and decided they'd go home and write up everything bad they could think of and put it in the mail. That bothered me. When you have that big hatchet hanging over your head that could wind up costing you millions of dollars in penalties, it's not the best time to be out buying other properties. We decided not to buy the retirement home that was in trouble. It turned out that the people who did buy it made several million dollars in a matter of months.

The thing you have to keep in mind is not just how much the IRS says you owe or how much you wind up paying them. *It's how much you have to pay the people that defend you—which wound up being millions of dollars for me— and it's what it can do to you and your family personally.* You go to bed every night wondering if you'll wake up in the morning and the IRS will shoot you. People will say that's farfetched, but they haven't been where I've been. I thought I had done well and done things right and people had always told me that. But then a couple of people that wound up retiring as soon as they quit messing with us started telling me that I did wrong. The only good thing was that since they retired, maybe instead of them driving us crazy, we drove them crazy.

When they would send us a report on what they had found, there would usually be about five paragraphs on a page. When we answered the report, I can hardly remember a paragraph that didn't begin with, "What the examiner does not understand is..." or "What the examiner did wrong was..." We had to explain things to them like a little child. It was really bad. The record will show that.

It bothers me to think about how much we lost in earnings during this period. You can lose a lot of deals in nine or ten years, and you go through a lot of boom cycles that you're missing. You're afraid to spend the money that you have because you're afraid they may say that you owe them some.

It changes your whole way of thinking and lifestyle. It can even affect your personality. It's hard getting up in the morning knowing that they might close down your bank account with no notice or take the stuff out of your house. Anyone that says the IRS would never do things like that has never been through it. Occasionally when they have a hearing on Capitol Hill about the IRS, some of my friends will say, "Aw, they couldn't be that bad." Yes they can, and if you've been through it, you know that they can.

I'd try to whistle and act like it was no big deal, but we were losing opportunities left and right. I'd go out to my farm and ride the tractor and hear the birds sing and all of a sudden I'd remember that foreign guy that couldn't speak English and only spoke IRS. It really put a damper on things.

My wife and family stayed very strong throughout the whole ordeal. When you go to church and you know you haven't done anything wrong, even though it bothers you, you still know that they can't send you to the big burial ground. You've always got something to fall back on. That's the way my family looked at it. People kept saying, "Well, it will make you stronger." If I had gotten any stronger, I don't think I could have stood it. We just kept hanging in there.

Finally, they tidied up all their mess and made up all the penalties they could possibly think of. They sent it off in a big package to the district office. I was hopeful that this was where we would get some justice, because at least they spoke English at the district office. They're supposed to be more qualified.

A key point to all this is that it started in 1988, so they were supposed to be able to go back to 1985 to look at records. This was 1992. That's seven years worth of records, which you would think would be enough. Nope. They've got them a real system, and it's called "extensions." They send you a letter that says, "You can give us a voluntary extension or we'll shoot you." You either do what they say, which means they're still thinking about it, or you can choose not to give them an extension, and they'll write down everything bad they can think of. I bet they've got a book up there that says, "Boilerplate book: when everything else fails, charge them with this." They go through the book and pick out crazy stuff to charge. We wound up with over twenty things they were accusing us of.

We had the best people money could buy helping us and the other side was so incompetent that our people couldn't understand them. One time we decided we were going to get even better people. We hired a guy from a law firm in Washington and he was supposed to be the dean of attorneys. He had experience with the IRS and he was going to fly to Raleigh and meet with us. I thought, "Now we're getting somewhere. We're going to get somebody in here that's going to solve everything."

I met the man at the airport. He was one of the nicest guys in the world. I hauled him downtown to the place we had our meetings. He kept going on about how nice it was for me to pick him up so that he wouldn't have to catch a cab. I thought, "I hired him. Why wouldn't I pick him up? I'd have picked up my dog at the airport, so why wouldn't I pick him up?"

When we got downtown and went through the stuff, I came to realize that in his mind, his mission was to convince me that no matter how right I was, fairness was not the way the IRS worked. They weren't going to be happy until they extracted some blood from me. *I felt like telling him that we were still fighting, we weren't giving up. I didn't hire him to show me how to throw in the towel.* But he felt like after they had spent so much time going after me, they were going to wind up getting something. I guess he had a point. They had more help than we did. We had a library, but heck, they had the Library of Congress.

Still, we weren't ready to quit. I finally convinced him to fight more than he had wanted to fight. We wrote a good stiff report and sent it back. I took him back to the airport. We stopped at Golden Corral on the way and sat there eating a steak. He said, "I want to tell you one more time how nice it was to bring me back to the airport. Most people tell me to find my own way back. It must be Southern hospitality."

I said, "Shucks no. I've just never seen a man eat that made $375 an hour. I wanted to see if you chewed differently from me or something."

We wound up becoming pretty good friends. I think he became convinced that we were serious about what we were doing. We weren't trying to buy our way out the cheapest way possible.

Finally, all our stuff got sent back up to Greensboro to the district office. We could talk a lot about what each case was about, but that's not important. The key point is that we won just about every single thing that was contested. The only thing we lost was relating to what I was getting paid, which had to do with wages reclassified and depreciation. It wasn't that we were wrong; it was just a matter of opinion about how to do things. Their opinion probably would've been the same as ours if they hadn't needed to find something that they could win and squeeze a few dollars from.

"The dollars we gave them had nothing to do with right and wrong," my accountant, James A. Lucas, Jr., said. "It was strictly a timing issue. They were going to get the money no matter what. We had a difference of opinion on whether it was proper to get it now, then, or later. That was the only thing they got, and they would've gotten it whether they started the whole proceeding or not."

Eventually, we made it to the regional director of appeals in the middle of 1993. We thought we were going to get some justice. But it dragged on into 1994 and we still hadn't heard anything. They had a real funny idea of what it meant to play fair. They would go off and take several months to do something, and all of a sudden they'd pop up and say they needed something from us in two weeks.

One year they notified us on December 17th that they needed a bunch of records by December 31st. Where I come from, that's everyone's Christmas break. I guess they thought Santa Claus would bring it or something. Oh, sure, it's no problem to dig through ten-year-old records and find something in two weeks. We asked them about what was going on when we still hadn't heard anything, and they said, "Oh, we meant to tell you. We're just overloaded up here, and your case has been transferred to the New Orleans office." I don't know whether they were overworked or not, but I'm sure they thought if they sent us far enough away that we'd quit bothering them.

Naturally, we couldn't find out anything from New Orleans. We kept calling and calling and never heard anything. In late 1994, we discovered that the case never even went to New Orleans. It was still in Greensboro. We called the man in charge at Greensboro and he said he thought they might start working on it pretty soon. He called a few days later and said there was something he didn't understand and he'd have to send it up to Washington for some advice.

I wanted to tell him that we had already won up there one time and we didn't mind going back. We'd like to get another win up there if it wasn't for all the time we'd have to spend on it. I really think that their main strategy is to wear you out. They thought we'd give in and pay them something. But they didn't count on me not wearing out easy.

At the very end of 1994, we had to send all our people up to Washington again. We heard that they were thinking about ruling against us, so we sent all our people up there to meet with them for a second time. In 1995, they sent a letter from Washington down to Greensboro that said, "What you sent us had no basis and your request to rule against Mr. Ammons is denied. If the case were litigated, the taxpayer would most likely prevail. Therefore, we withdraw our request for a ruling." They didn't say that I was right or wrong. They didn't say it was fair. They didn't say, "We're sorry for screwing with Jud and for wasting all his time." They just said they thought that we would win.

We thought this meant it was over. They had said we were going to win. But no, they decided they wanted to start all over. No matter what you give them, they always seem to want more information. It might be bragging, but it's the truth: they never were able to prove that we hid one single dollar. Our records were always, always exactly as we had said they were.

They don't have any accountability. I had learned back when I was a kid and bought those stunted pigs that if you did something wrong, you should accept the consequences and admit you were wrong. If I had acted like the IRS when I bought those pigs, I would've gone back to the man that sold them to me and told him that he owed me thirty more healthy pigs and made up some rule that told him he had to pay me what I wanted. Instead, I admitted that I was wrong. The IRS doesn't know how to do that. It's difficult to teach your kids about accountability when the government doesn't even know what the word means.

Finally, in 1995, the local office sent the case back to the Greensboro office once again. This was 1995. We're talking about years, not days. Much of the stuff that was up for discussion had happened a decade ago. In the meantime, they'd decided they'd audit another company of ours that wasn't even in Raleigh. It was in Wilmington, several hundred miles away. I guess they thought if we were going to hide something, we'd hide it way off where we didn't know anybody.

The IRS sent the nicest agent down there to check out things. He was a different auditor from a different district. If they had sent him out to see us on the first day in 1988, we might've been able to finish in less than ten years. He spent one day looking at our stuff and issued a report within ten days. It was a no-change report, and he commented that our records were right and that he admired the way we kept everything in order. Of course, that seemed to bother the people that were after us even more.

They figured that if they were going to get Mr. Ammons they had to paddle their own wagon. By now, we were up to 1996. It was becoming pretty evident that the people in the Greensboro office didn't want to settle anything unless they got a little bit of money. We had already been proven right more than once and I still had my principles. It was a double-edged sword. We could either give up and give the local yo-yo's something or we could risk this thing dragging on into the next millennium.

Letting it drag on had quite a few potential side effects. Even though I tried not to let it bother me and tried to keep going about my business, the banks didn't look at it exactly the same way. We had one deal that was in the tens of millions of dollars. The bank wrote us a letter using words such as, "Outstanding project," "Fine reputation," "Every reason to be proud." Then you get to the big "however." I really wish they would take that word out of the English language. It's screwed up more good things than anything else in the world.

Anyway, the bank said, "However, it's impossible to move ahead given the uncertainty of the contingency of the IRS." That meant that since the IRS said we owed them millions of dollars, it didn't matter what the truth was. It bothered them enough that they didn't make us the loan and we weren't able to do the project. Sooner or later, some IRS screwball is going to figure out that if they will leave us alone and let us make more money, we'll have to give them more. So far, they haven't figured it out yet.

Finally, the day came that I had to decide if I was going to give up on some of my principles. All the people that were advising me told me that no one was able to win one hundred percent against the IRS, no matter how clean they were. Even Jesus couldn't have won one hundred percent against them.

We decided to give in on two issues. One of them involved how much I had paid myself. The other was an issue of depreciation. We'd already proved that we did it correctly within one dollar, but that wasn't enough for them. It's worth pointing out here that this was before the days when I had a computer, so everything we proved in these millions of dollars we did on a yellow sheet of paper with a pencil. It was no small task. But, we decided it would be in our best interests to change some of the depreciation and give the IRS a little bit of money. The little bit we gave them was nowhere near the amount I spent defending myself. It wasn't even close. And the funny part was they couldn't even say we did anything wrong. All they did was change a deduction from one year to the other year. It was just a question of which year we got the deduction in.

But if everything we had gone through didn't take the cake, there was more to come. We thought we were going

to be totally through with them. They said, "Yeah, we think so." Think so? Huh? I tried to write them a check that said, "Paid in full." They said they didn't take that kind of check. They couldn't give us a letter that said we had settled the case or that they would leave us alone. They said they had to have the option to come back and get us if they got the urge.

We wanted a closing letter, which would say everything that happened and that the Ammons Saga was now finished. The IRS said they couldn't do it. When the lawyers and everyone told me that, my reply was, "Tell that son of a bitch I'm not going to sign anything." They tried to persuade me and said the agent was being halfway decent about it, mostly because he was getting ready to retire (One thing I learned—when those agent guys got close to us, it pushed them closer to retirement. This was about the third or fourth guy that had gotten out right after dealing with us). I eventually agreed with them.

What do you think the chances of them coming back and getting me are? The agent said it was slim because they were going to figure up the whole case in Memphis. That's apparently where they keep their gigantic smart people and the computer that knows all. Memphis was supposed to end the whole thing.

We thought they were a thing of the past. In 1997, we were back to business as usual. I got a call about six months later from a guy that I was doing a little business with that said, "Mr. Ammons, your check bounced."

We aren't used to our checks bouncing. I couldn't believe it. I called the bank to see what in the world was going on. They said, "Oh, we sent you a letter three days ago." I never got the letter, so I asked them to fax it over. I pulled it out of the machine and this is what it said:

"Greetings. You have been chosen to have your bank account frozen. When we did our settlement six months ago, you didn't pay us everything that we were owed."

How can you ever go to sleep when you know that if they get a chance, they'll shoot you in the back?

We were ready to get this thing truly and finally over. My accountant found this nice lady who was in the business of solving things. She worked in the Problem Resolution Office, and God knows we had a problem, so she was perfect. After about ten days we had finally gotten our bank account unfrozen. Some people said we should be happy that we got it unfrozen that quickly. I thought it was ten days too long. I still remember one of the best comments the IRS ever made. Their agent said, "We can't find where Mr. Ammons owes this money, either. But it's in the computer, so unless you prove it to us otherwise, you have to pay it."

They can't even figure right. One time they were trying to figure and got the whole thing fouled up. We had to refigure it for them to show how much we owed. That's pretty bad, when the taxpayer has to show the IRS how to figure their charges. If you hired a lawyer and you wound up having to show them how to do everything in court, you would think they were pretty incompetent, wouldn't you?

So, now we were dealing with a machine. We had started in 1988, and here we were in 1997 trying to teach the IRS how to get our information out of their computer. They asked us if we had any suggestions, and my main one was to burn the thing down to the ground. That didn't go over too well.

At this point we were dealing with several thousand dollars instead of several million, so we decided to pay it instead of trying to convince the computer that we were right. If you've ever tried to convince a computer that it is wrong, you know that you don't get too far with that.

After we paid it, we started thinking that the IRS must owe us at least a little bit of money. We started looking for someone that could get the information out of the computer and we wound up talking to the regional director in Greensboro. My accountant had been talking for me, my lawyer had been talking for me, and I was ready to speak for myself.

I went to Greensboro and had a meeting. I thought he was a really nice guy. It appeared to me that he was listening and he seemed to understand all that we had gone through. Come to think of it, he was getting ready to retire, too. We really must wear on people. He never promised us exactly what he would do, but he promised that he would go back and check the figures and personally see if we had been done wrong. I thought that was great. He didn't guarantee us what the results would be, but he at least said he would work on it.

Raleigh is a couple hours away, and all the way back from Greensboro we talked about how great it was that we had finally found a decent human being that did things fairly. We must have been hoping for too much, though. There was a message on my machine from him when I got home that said, "I can't do any of those things that I promised. Don't call me back. Bye." We did call him back a time or two trying to see if he had a conscience, but never got any response. We were still batting 1.000. We had found nobody that in my opinion had a conscience.

That quote from the judge at the beginning of this chapter was exactly right. It's not about fairness or right and wrong. Every time we would win, I never once heard anyone say they were sorry. I tried to talk to a Senator and a Congressman, and they were never any help.

One thing they did shortly after this was come up with the "Taxpayer Bill of Rights." I had a Congressman call me up and tell me how great this new idea was. I had already seen it and I told him it wasn't worth the paper it was printed on. Anyone that has any sense that studies it will realize it does them no good. It sounds good. Clinton likes it almost as much as he likes interns. But it says nothing. Our government has proven time and time again that the main thing they know how to do is have hearings, not solve problems.

Many people think that if you make money it's OK to have these problems. But as we've mentioned elsewhere, I'm already paying more than my share of the taxes. Those people are just interested in getting my money and they don't care if they get it fairly or unfairly.

I finally wound up paying 2.75% of the tax and penalties that were assessed against me. That was money that I'll get back at a later date. We only paid it as a timing issue. But it cost me much more than 2.75% in paying the people that helped me, in lost deals, and stress on my family. If I can think of anything good that came out of it, it's that my children got to see how the government operates. I hope that people who read this will know that it's not a pie-in-the-sky bunch of ridiculousness. It really did happen. I saw it firsthand and lived through every day of it. It really affects people's lives.

I was lucky, because I could afford to fight them and try and get them to treat me right. If I hadn't been able to fight them, I would've had to just give up in the second year and give them whatever they wanted.

Chapter 11
And So...

To The Men In The Arena

"It is not the critic who counts, not the man who points out how the strong man stumbles, or where the doer of deeds could have done them better.

The credit belongs to the man who is actually in the arena, whose face is marred by dust and sweat and blood, who strives valiantly, who errs and who comes short again and again, who knows the great enthusiasms, the great devotions and spends himself in a worthy cause, who at the best

knows the triumphs of high achievement, and who at the worst, if he fails, at the least fails while daring greatly, so that his place shall never be among those cold and timid souls who know neither pity nor defeat."

—Teddy Roosevelt

It's always bothered me that it seems like nobody wanted to take much of a risk. Everyone wanted to live in a way that they could be sure of what would happen to them forever. But there's several ways that people can take a risk. They can do it in their business, in finding their girlfriend, or in almost anything in life. But then we have the legal profession that wants to sue everyone to take the risk out. If you get a cup of coffee and spill it on you, they want to sue because that was a risk you shouldn't have had to endure. Well, if you're dumb enough not to know that coffee is hot, then maybe you got what you deserved.

We're in a search for a risk-free society. *But by doing that, we may risk everything: our liberty, a standard of living, and decreasing choices just by not taking risk.* We have a wonderful system of free enterprise. Since people came over on the *Mayflower*, if they've wanted to build something better and sell it for more, then that was possible. That's free enterprise. I guess I believe in it more than most people. It seems to me that we're trying to take all the risk out of that system. When that happens, we are in danger of losing our pioneering spirit. It's so tremendously important to be a real pioneer.

I always felt like I was cheated in life because I wasn't able to be a cowboy, or in on the Gold Rush, or a part of the wildcatters that were drilling for oil. I missed those magic times. But when you think about it, we're living in a magic time. Our country has had eight or nine years of prosperity, but people still don't want to take a risk. That means that there's just that much more opportunity for risk-takers. Instead of worrying about what we missed, maybe we're right in the middle of a good time period.

People say, "Gosh, Jud, you paid $250 an acre for that land and you sold it for $6,000. Wow, we wish we could do that." Well, if they could buy it for $6,000 an acre today, they might be able to sell it for $36,000 an acre in fifteen years. But it's easier to look at what someone else did instead of getting out and doing it themselves.

When we start a new development, as we're doing now in Mars Hill, a key decision is how much we're going to pioneer and how much we're just going to do the regular thing. We want to be as far out in front as possible as long as we're not broke. But then the sad fact is that as much as people talk about wanting to be on the cutting edge, when they're ready to buy a house they want four bedrooms, columns on the front, and a rumpus room over the garage. Oh yeah, that's real cutting edge.

Several years ago, I built the solar house at N.C. State. Everyone thought that was going to be a big deal in the future. It was more trouble than people wanted to go to, though. It's hard to push people to use new building techniques such as more solar heat.

I want to make things as pretty and cutting-edge as possible. But it's a fact that if you can't make money doing those things. You can't do it. So then you have a situation where you want to be innovative but you also want to make some money, and those two things don't jive. *The goal is to make enough money to stay in business while still building something that is as pretty, environmentally sensitive, and innovative enough that it's something to be proud of.*

Over the next ten or twenty years Andy is doing a project in Wake Forest that will involve him building several thousand houses and spending millions of dollars. He's going to spend more than fifty percent of his time satisfying some level of government. If they'd just leave him alone, with no rules, it would be much more efficient and certainly better and more economically feasible for the buyers and a better place to live.

Most people wouldn't agree. They think they need the government to protect them. But that's not who should provide the protection. You're supposed to protect yourself.

It's like when I bought those pigs—if I didn't know enough to buy, I shouldn't have bought. If I had bought those pigs in 1999, there probably would've been some Pig-Buying Association of America that would've filed a lawsuit on my behalf and wanted to stage a protest. There are too many people that it's possible to ask and find out information about what you're buying. The government doesn't have to tell you those things.

I suppose I have so much respect for our buyers and consumers in general that I think they know enough to look out for themselves. I believe they have enough sense to decide what they want to buy and how much they want to pay for it. It's not up to someone else to tell them. I would rather sit down with buyers, get to know them, and work together to make their house like they want it.

When I came along, most people lived on the farm. I heard someone say that the first time we would be in real trouble was when we were three generations away from the farm. That might seem backwards to some people, but I think what was meant was that we might lose our rural heritage and the strong work ethic. Back then, people just believed in working harder. We were proud of being able to work more and share more. Today, people just want to live for themselves and forget everyone else.

If we did something wrong, we paid the price. Blaming something else never crossed our mind. These days, there's a whole host of excuses. It was the way they grew up, or their parents, or all those things. It sure was simpler when we were responsible for our own actions. I hear a lot of parents today say that they're worried their kids won't be as responsible as they want them to be. With the kind of government we have in our society, that's a reasonable worry.

With the blessings of the welfare system, we have a system of entitlements. Entitlement is a funny word to me.

I always thought that everyone was entitled to what they earned. They weren't entitled to anything based on what they looked like or how tall they were or how smart they were.

By bringing in a welfare system, we've taken out anything having to do with people sharing and helping each other on their own initiative. If you don't believe it, go to a meeting of any homeowners' association. Everyone lives in the same neighborhood and pays a little bit of money to the association. Say that there's a lake in the development. Well, the people that live on the lake want to spend twice as much to make the lake pretty. The ones that don't want to live on the lake but have to walk down to look at it don't want to spend a dollar on the lake. Everyone is looking out for himself. It has nothing to do with what makes a better community.

Our welfare system tries to figure out who is in need so that we can give them something for free. The qualifiers for the free stuff get put on a list. In some schools, if you can get a certain percentage of people on the list, you get more federal money. So that forces you to go out and try to convince people that they're in need so that they can go on the list. If someone told me I was on a poor list, I think I'd go hungry until I could get off of it.

At the same time, we wonder what happened to self-esteem. We have to have "social promotions" in school so that kids won't feel bad about themselves. How do we expect them to feel good if we want them to be proud of being on the poor list and getting free stuff? It shouldn't be something to be proud of. But most people aren't even bothered by being on that list.

When people start getting something for free, it's easy to get used to it. When all of a sudden it's not there, they wonder what happened to it. A whole generation is growing up wondering who they can blame for their problems.

We wonder why kids bring a gun to school. The politicians want to say that it's because it's easier to find a gun. There are fewer guns per capita in 1999 than there have been in fifteen years. You don't hear that statistic very much, because it's a fact that gets in the way of the political arguments. No one will believe this because it's not what the politicians say, but it's twice as hard to get a gun now as it was twenty-five years ago. Back then anyone could walk down to the corner store and buy as many as they wanted.

The problems we're having aren't because of the quantity of guns. They're because in today's society we don't teach kids right and wrong and that there can be repercussions to doing something wrong.

In the last four years, North Carolina has issued almost 50,000 permits for people to carry a guy or have a concealed weapon. In all that time, no one has used one of those guns to commit a felony. Our government can go into Waco like a Rambo movie and all those people die, but they cover it up by lying about it. A lot of people were upset with what happened in Waco, as we saw by the Oklahoma City bombing. It's not too big a stretch to say that our government caused what happened in Oklahoma.

If our president does bad things and lies about them, why shouldn't we expect the same from our government? When we have school shootings, everyone from the president on down wants to blame it on guns. No one ever wants to take responsibility, not even the parents. We shouldn't expect anything different. Personal responsibility and setting a good example went down the drain a long time ago.

I don't know where we will go from here. I don't think anyone knows. But wouldn't it be nice if everyone decided today that from this point on we were all going to do our part? We weren't going to complain about who wasn't doing their part. We could decide that we wanted a more efficient system, so that we could make more out of the resources we have. No more suing each other for stupid stuff. No more twenty-five or thirty page contracts to buy a house. I can remember when having a two-page contract was considered a little flaky because everyone wanted a one-page.

I'm sure that it looks like I don't have any hope, but I do. I see my grandkids and other grandkids, the high school students that my wife and I have in our Sunday school class, and the kids that went on the mission trip with me. That gives me hope. If things get bad enough, maybe we'll all decide that it's time to buckle down and get to business. Maybe everyone will decide they want to do their share. And that's what gives me hope.

I don't know any story that sums up more of what I think has happened to America than one that was told by George McGovern. He was a Senator for a number of years and eventually decided to run for President. I remember thinking that if he got elected, it would be one of the worst things that ever happened. I couldn't imagine that anyone could be worse for the country than him. He thought the government should put you to bed at night and wake you up in the morning. Maybe that's a little harsh, but I think it was generally agreed that he was among the most liberal of his time. I'm sure he was a kind and gentle person that loved people, but he was totally wrong.

As we know, he didn't get elected President, and he went back to New England. He wanted to realize his lifetime dream of owning a restaurant or a bed-and-breakfast, so he went into business. After some time, he went bankrupt. He couldn't get permits for different elements and couldn't meet the requirements that were set up by the government agencies.

He wrote an article that was published in Nation's Building News in 1992. In it, he wrote, "I wish that during the years I was in public office, I had had this firsthand experience about the difficulties business people face every day. That knowledge would have made me a better U.S. Senator and a more understanding presidential contender...I lived with federal, state, and local rules that were all passed with the objective of helping employees, protecting the environment, raising tax dollars for schools, protecting our customers from fire hazards, etc. While I never have doubted the worthiness of any of these goals, the concept that most often eludes legislators is: 'Can we make consumers pay the higher prices for the increased operating costs that accompany public regulation and government reporting requirements with reams of red tape.' It is a simple concern that is nonetheless often ignored by legislators." I give him a lot of credit for saying that. Most people can't admit when they're wrong.

It would be great if we never had teachers that tried to teach something they'd never done on their own. The less professional politicians we have in this world, the better off we will be. They don't know what it's like to lay awake at night and wonder if someone is going to come take away their house. If no one that had never been there had any authority, the world would be a better place.

Chapter 12
Don't Wish You Had,
Be Glad You Did

Someone once said that a life shouldn't be judged by how much money you make or your social standing. They said it should be judged by what your children do for others. My wife says that I shouldn't talk too much about this, because people will think I'm bragging. But as important as the kids are to me and as proud as I am of them, I think it's important. On the first page, I said I was writing this for my grandchildren. If that's the case, I want them to know about their parents and all that they've accomplished.

Several years ago, my daughter went with her church to work at a homeless shelter. She met a girl who was around twenty or twenty-one and had a little year-old daughter. They really got along, and Alma couldn't understand why she would be in a homeless shelter. It seemed like she had just had a run of bad luck and needed a little bit of opportunity.

Alma took the girl home with her and let her stay at her house for a couple weeks until they could work something out. The Sunday school class donated a little bit of money and some people helped her buy a car. After a couple weeks the lady was able to move out into an apartment and get a job. It's hard for me to talk about without crying.

All of our children and their spouses have done the same type of thing. They've helped in shelters or in food kitchens, been President of the PTA, been a deacon in the church, worked with the deaf ministry, taught Sunday school, and participated in professional organizations and civic clubs. None have slacked off any, even though they could have.

I hope that I've had something to do with it. When I get to thinking about it, I wonder if maybe my parents and grandparents didn't have even more to do with it. I still remember taking my eighty-six-year-old grandfather to his former church in order for him to preach the Homecoming sermon. Both his legs had been amputated, but he was still working with the church. They're the ones that set an example for me. In turn, Jo Ellen and I have tried to set an example for the kids. As they got bigger, maybe they didn't want to get up early and go to Easter sunrise service or something like that. Once they got older, we didn't make them do it if they didn't feel like it was important. But we always got up and went. They may not have gone, but I bet they felt bad about it. The next time, maybe they went. And today, they all go. They were able to decide on their own that it was important for them to do that type of thing.

We had so many people set good examples for us: teachers, family members, and a host of others. When you have people like that behind you, it really means something.

The other day, Andy was talking about how much money he was going to owe because of starting this new development. "I'm concerned," he said. "Pretty soon, I'm going to be owing in the millions of dollars. What do you think about that?"

I looked at him and I said, "I think that sounds like a good start." You don't want to be chicken. No way. If he had been chicken, I would have felt like a complete flop.

Another thing we've tried to teach them is to treat people like they want to be treated. Can you imagine how great it would be if everyone did that? But when we're talking about paying for new schools or anything like that, everyone wants someone else to pay. The people that have lived here a long time want the new people to pay. The new people want the older residents to pay.

One time, I was on the planning board. A lady came down and strongly opposed a rezoning near the outside of town. They were rezoning a big horse farm into four or five acre mini-horse farms. She lived on that type of farm. She didn't even live on the big one, but she thought it was pretty. I asked her how long she had lived where she lived, and she said, "Two years ago. I moved from New Jersey."

I told her that I remembered when a man had come in and gotten the land she lived on rezoned into mini-farms. If he hadn't done that, she couldn't have lived where she lived. Her reply was, "I don't see that that has anything to do with it."

Well, if she didn't see the relationship between the two, there wasn't much sense in having a conversation. She wanted her cake and wanted to eat it too. Pure selfishness.

• • •

I hope I'm not too old or tired to do a lot more pretty things. There are so many potential projects out there. Some people think we do it for the money, but that couldn't be further from the truth. You have to make money to stay in the business, but that's not why you do it. It's a challenge to see how pretty you can make it. When we started Nags Head, I had never built anything on a pile of sand before. What could be more fun than that? If I can, I want to keep doing that.

It's pretty obvious that we don't do it for the money. If I go out and make $100 and leave it for my grandchildren, they will get less than $10. So why keep doing projects? Someone else is going to get all the money eventually. So we're obviously not doing it just for that.

It's so important to dream and soar. Some people want to sit down and make a detailed plan before they ever start something. They get so caught up in the planning that they forget to start. While you're living, you've got to live. Don't wish you had, be glad you did.

Jud-isms

"I know I can live with being broke. But I can't live with thinking I was being a chicken."

"The know how isn't nearly as important as the want-to."

"It's important to try and make some money. Dividing up something is never a problem, but dividing up nothing is always tough."

"You can't get greedy and price yourself out of the market."

"Momentum is not too hard to get, but the hardest thing in the world to get back when you lose it."

"It's hard to do anything if you never get up the courage to start."

"The way to get along with some people is to let them think they've won something."

"Don't wish you had, be glad you did."

"Every day is not the Alamo."

"Where two or more are gathered, there is one in every crowd."

"To find the answer follow the money trail."

"Some are born in gear, and some out of gear. Not many with a clutch."

"Bad times don't last, but good men do."